Mark Wigan

TEXT AND IMAGE

n. a subject or theme

n. a representation,
an image or conception

ava Academia
the environment of learning

An AVA Book
Published by AVA Publishing SA
Rue des Fontenailles 16
Case Postale
1000 Lausanne 6
Switzerland
Tel: +41 786 005 109
Email: enquiries@avabooks.ch

Distributed by Thames & Hudson (ex-North America)
181a High Holborn
London WC1V 7QX
United Kingdom
Tel: +44 20 7845 5000
Fax: +44 20 7845 5055
Email: sales@thameshudson.co.uk
www.thamesandhudson.com

Distributed in the USA & Canada by:
Watson-Guptill Publications
770 Broadway
New York, New York 10003
USA
Fax: +1 646 654 5487
Email: info@watsonguptill.com
www.watsonguptill.com

English Language Support Office
AVA Publishing (UK) Ltd.
Tel: +44 1903 204 455
Email: enquiries@avabooks.co.uk

ISBN 2-940373-50-7 and 978-2-940373-50-5

10 9 8 7 6 5 4 3 2 1

Design by Littlefire Design
Original text and photography by Mark Wigan

Production by
AVA Book Production Pte. Ltd., Singapore
Tel: +65 6334 8173
Fax: +65 6259 9830
Email: production@avabooks.com.sg

All reasonable attempts have been made to trace,
clear and credit the copyright holders of the images
reproduced in this book. However, if any credits have
been inadvertently omitted, the publisher will endeavour
to incorporate amendments in future editions.

Table of contents

Introduction   06
How to get the most out of this book   10

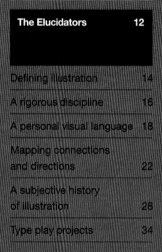

The Elucidators   12

Interpretation   36

**Text, Images, Ideas
and Messages**   60

Defining illustration   14

A rigorous discipline   16

A personal visual language   18

Mapping connections
and directions   22

A subjective history
of illustration   28

Type play projects   34

Amplifying the text   38

Author/illustrator   42

The visual journalist   46

Book art   50

Narrative illustration
projects   58

Editorial illustration   62

Conceptual image-making   66

Persuasive image-making   70

To instruct and inform   74

Text as image and
image as text   78

Letterform projects   82

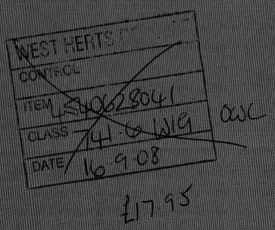

A Myriad of Platforms	84
Poster design	86
Magazines	90
Installation and interventions	100
Book jackets	106
Text in motion	110
Visual impact projects	114

Illustrative Text	116
Magical letterforms	118
Handcrafted type	122
Sampling and mixing	130
Typographic poetry	136
Handmade type projects	140

Graphic Art Zeitgeist	142
Sound and vision	144
Image, music and text	146
Club flyers	152
Zeitgeist projects	156

Conclusion	158
Glossary	160
Illustration Dialogues	162
Reference Material	166
Influential Posters and Record Sleeves	170
Contacts	172
Acknowledgements and Picture Credits	176

Table of contents

TEATB WIELKI

Title
Teatr Wielki
(Alban Berg Wozzeck)
Illustrator
Jan Lenica
Description
Offset lithograph
poster (c.1964)

ALBAN BERG WOZZECK

Illustrators are visual communicators and picture-makers who construct meaning and convey ideas, narratives, messages and emotions to specific audiences, readers and users. Fundamental to this process is personal creative expression, the pleasure and sheer enjoyment of creative image-making and the interpretation of words and ideas into images. Illustration has been defined as the amplifying, elucidating, adorning, illuminating, decorating, enhancing and extending of the text. As such illustration is much more than a literal translation of the text; it can be allusive and function as an oblique counterpoint to the copy.

Basics Illustration: Text and Image explores the interpretation of words into pictures and the interplay of text and images in both a wide range of media and in historical, contemporary, social, economic, political, cultural and critical contexts. This book seeks to further explore the art and craft of illustration and the fundamental relationship between text and image in order to provide inspiration and encourage discovery with an extremely wide range of visual languages, theories, creative processes, techniques, methodologies, visual solutions and points of view.

Basic principles of graphic communication are introduced and both historical and cutting edge contemporary examples are analysed and contextualised in order to inspire, inform and stimulate. As students of illustration, you will be encouraged to discover the way meaning is formed by text and image, the underlying semiological basis of the work featured, and to develop an awareness of how images directly or subconsciously affect their users and audiences.

The illustrator's domain is the personal and the idiosyncratic; they are sympathetic to the emotion and rhythm of words, making appropriate and effective use of visual language. Illustrations can be life-affirming, absurd, coherent, intelligent, beguiling, incisive and visceral; they are signs and symbols manipulated to persuade, provoke, amuse, inform, entertain or educate.

Text and image are two forms of representation; two visual signs that can integrate and reinforce one another to communicate messages, emotions, ideas or visual commentary. Words and pictures can be employed to challenge one another, separating and countering meaning; text subverting the image and vice versa.

There is a huge resurgence in illustration; the discipline is evolving and flourishing. At the forefront of this activity a new wave of illustrators are following their own voices, extending their role beyond that of decorators, space fillers and servants to the text. *Text and Image* analyses and explores the relationships, synergies, and the blurring of boundaries between illustration and other creative disciplines.

Teatr Wielki (left)

Jan Lenica (1928–2001) blurred borders and crossed genres. Lenica felt that a poster must 'sing'. This is evident in his Teatr Wielki poster. Designed for an opera, it features reverberating 'screams' emanating from concentric circles.

Chapter One: The Elucidators

This chapter charts a cross-disciplinary and eclectic chronology of text and image. It maps connections and directions in a constantly changing world of audiences, interventions and cultural, theoretical and ideological contexts.

Chapter Two: Interpretation

This chapter contains idiosyncratic reflections on the interpretive art of illustration. It explores how words can be amplified into images and convey emotions, ideas, messages and stories. The concept of the illustrator as author and visual journalist is also discussed.

Chapter Three: Text, Images, Ideas and Messages

In this chapter a variety of graphic media, genres and artefacts are contextualised. Illustrators present their own diverse techniques, methodologies, visual languages and insights into professional practice and current debates.

Chapter Four: A Myriad of Platforms

A wide range of graphic genres and media are introduced here including posters, magazines, comics, installations, book jackets and moving text and image. Featured artefacts include examples from *Zoom*, *LE GUN* and *The Illustrated Ape*.

Chapter Five: Illustrative Text

This chapter explores the integration and manipulation of text as image. Historical information is supported by contemporary case studies, points of view, personal working methodologies and professional and theoretical contexts. Themes explored include handcrafted type, collage and typographic poetry.

Chapter Six: Graphic Art Zeitgeist

This chapter introduces contemporary hybridised practice, such as sound and vision work, music promotion and packaging and club flyers.

Title
Intuitive doodle
Illustrator
Jon Burgerman
Description
Limited-edition print

Introduction

How to get the most out of this book

This book introduces different aspects of text and image via dedicated chapters for each topic. Each chapter provides numerous examples of work by leading artists, with interview quotes to explain their rationales, methodologies and working processes. Key illustration principles are isolated so that the reader can see how they are applied in practice.

Clear navigation
Each chapter section has a clear running head to allow readers to quickly locate areas of interest.

Introductions
Special section introductions outline basic concepts that will be discussed.

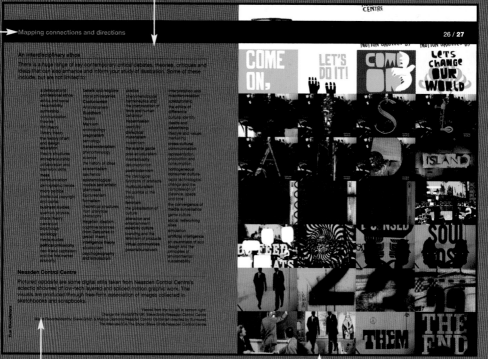

Related information
Related information, such as historical precedents and term definitions are also included.

Examples
Commercial projects from contemporary illustrators visually bring the principles under discussion alive.

Written explanations

Key points are explained
and placed in context.

Editorial illustration

62 / 63

Traditional editorial illustration tends to cover work for lifestyle magazines, colour supplements, journals, in-house corporate magazines and regional or national newspapers. But contemporary editorial illustrators are commissioned to convey messages and clarify content in a wide range of contexts and for a variety of outlets.

One of these is book publishing, which encompasses packaging, book jackets, fiction, non-fiction, educational, technical, specialist or showcase books, graphic novels, comics, and children's books. Other forms of commissions for editorial illustrators include below-the-line company reports, brochures, point-of-sale material, retail signage, websites, corporate identity designs, logotypes and exhibition design.

Editorial commissions sometimes require a series of images to be produced in the form of a visual essay. However, it's more usual for single images that employ concepts and metaphors and provide an alternative view that summarises and conveys the underlying meaning behind the text, to be commissioned for this market.

Traditional editorial illustration commissions have always provided vital employment for illustrators. However, factors that have had a recent impact on illustrators working in this market include competition from the increasing use of photographic visuals and designer-made digital collages, the transition from print to the internet as a source of immediate news information and an increasing awareness of the environmental cost of mass-produced printed media.

Magazine and newspaper circulations may be failing (as they are now just one form of numerous communication channels), but they continue to provide publishing opportunities for the visual messages, ideas and commentaries of illustrators. The resurgence of interest (or so-called renaissance) in illustration in recent years has led to an increase in illustrated commissions in areas such as advertising, fashion promotion, animation, comics, web design and editorial work. Magazines, newspapers and websites are now frequently opting to commission illustrations instead of photographs, but illustrators are also utilising digital cameras and incorporating photography into their work, thereby merging the two disciplines.

The worst thing that can be done is having the text say one thing and the image just repeating that. The image should comment on the text and vice versa. Then things become interesting.
Jonas Bergstrand

Title
Døden en Bekymring
Illustrator
Jonas Bergstrand
Description
Retro-style design

DØDEN EN BEKYMRING

TORGNY LINDGREN & ERIC ÅKERLUND

KRIMINALROMAN SAMLEREN

Quotes

Quotes from featured illustrators
and from artists throughout
history are included.

Additional information

Captions feature illustrator and
image information.

The Collector

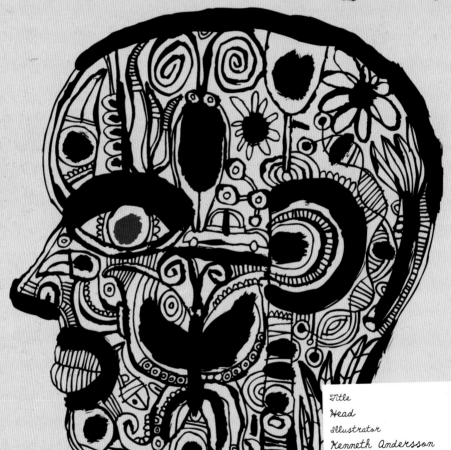

Title
Head
Illustrator
Kenneth Andersson
Description
Inspired by Outsider Art
in The Collector

As illustrators, we might often say that a picture is 'worth a thousand words', but we also need to ask what those words are, why they are being interpreted into images, for whom and for whose benefit.

The vast majority of illustration and graphic design artefacts could be considered trivial, trite, vacuous, derivative, formulaic and superficial. Combinations of text, images and ideas now saturate much of the world, promoting corporate consumer capitalism and brand recognition. It is now commonplace for illustrators and designers to be commissioned by corporate organisations in order to persuade consumers to buy goods and services by creating and responding to patterns of behaviour, aspirations, desires, motivations and needs. Commercial artists are now agents of consumption that manipulate signs, symbols and messages to educate, seduce, entertain and inform their specific target audiences.

But this corporate, brand-led and dominant production paradigm represents only one form of contemporary illustration and design practice in the 21st century. Many illustrators and designers are dissatisfied with playing the role of intermediary for mainstream global consumerism, and some are choosing to turn their backs on the design industry altogether, instead preferring to become contemporary artists exhibiting in galleries. Other practitioners are embracing a broader moral and ethical view of visual communication and are working to promote social engagement and change, supporting an idealistic and utopian view that the purpose of design is to create a better world for all and that visual communication is not just the effective, neutral and value-free conveying of the ideas and needs of others.

This chapter will:

explore the underlying social and cultural factors that have an impact on the discipline of illustration,

introduce examples of personal visual languages and map connections and directions within the subject,

review an attempt to provide a subjective history of illustration,

provide definitions of the discipline, examples of multidisciplinary contemporary practice and present a series of type play projects.

Head (left)

Kenneth Andersson is based in Sweden, where he has written and illustrated several children's books and worked on a range of print media, advertising and book-publishing projects. Andersson's work employs the use of varied qualities of line, produced first in ink (with pens and brushes) and then enhanced

Defining illustration

Any attempt to define illustration will invariably involve many different points of view. There are those who say it predates writing and began with cave paintings, whilst others say that it is a minor craft-based art that is inferior to fine art.

To some it can be a form of visual communication, or a problem-solving activity, or a means of social commentary or journalism. To others it can be an applied art in a commercial context, or a popular humane narrative art. For designers, it is often referred to as image-making; a specialism or adjunct of the hybrid discipline of graphic design. Finally, some claim that all contemporary art and design is in fact now illustration.

What makes this applied pictorial art so popular and interesting is that it fulfils the imperative to communicate, combining imagination, creativity, skill and craft to tell stories visually and invent new worlds. In the context of art and design education, illustration is the only area that still places fundamental importance on the acquisition of objective and observational drawing skills in order to underpin the creation of a personal visual language. At its best, illustration can be powerful, satirical, subversive, decorative, intimate, humorous, intelligent, allusive, inspiring, charming, beautiful, life-affirming and spiritually enriching.

Title
Portraits
Illustrator
Jason Atomic
Description
Clubland sketchbook

Title
Underground magazines and art school journals
Description
Courtesy of the Camberwell College of Arts library

A rigorous discipline

In the discipline of illustration, education should provide a student-centred, dynamic laboratory of ideas. Illustrators learn by a process of doing and making. Fundamental building blocks include visual literacy and perceptual skills and learning to look, see, draw and think. This deep approach to learning is not passive; it requires interaction and participation with others, imagination, commitment, problem-solving, communication, experimentation, a strong work ethic, constant and intense practice, collaboration, flexibility and an open-minded approach. Also key here are social and political concerns.

Social and political activism is a recurring thread in art and design history. It can be traced from street graffiti in ancient Rome to 16th-century chapbooks and 19th-century broadsheets and radical periodicals; throughout the Arts and Crafts, Futurist, Dadaist, Surrealist, Constructivist, Bauhaus and De Stijl movements to the propaganda posters, civil rights and anti-war protest graphics and punk fanzines of the 1960s and 1970s; and onto the more contemporary work of the Guerrilla Girls, street art, virtual micro-political global networks and *Adbusters* magazine.

Designers, artists and illustrators have always sought to change the world by assuming the role of graphic agitators, chroniclers, commentators, critics and the conscience of society. Self-reliant practitioners are now becoming authors and are establishing small illustrator/designer groups and networks that initiate, develop, publish and manufacture bespoke and handcrafted products, using entrepreneurial strategies to promote their personal projects.

Social, environmental and professional responsibility has now become a priority that underpins both the illustrator's choice of commercial and non-commercial projects and informs the negotiations and collaborations between illustrators, designers, clients and audiences. The idiosyncratic visual languages of illustrators provide empathy and emotive resonance for community-engaged information design projects and cultural, educational and issue-based campaigns. They address diverse social needs for a wide variety of audiences, employing persuasive advertising methods and engaging with subject matter such as poverty, human and animal rights, civil liberties, social inequality, homelessness, nuclear power, racism, sexism, ecological sustainability, global warming, disabilities and social inclusion.

The Elucidators

Title
Chairman Meow
Illustrator
Russell Walker
Description
Promotional playing card for the Central Illustration Agency

CHAIRMAN MEOW

A personal visual language

The study of illustration should take place outside the constraints and parameters of commerce and industry, and elements such as depth and breadth, experimentation, original ideas, content and the development of a personal direction and voice should be prioritised.

For the contemporary student of illustration, cultural and political awareness, critical practice and theoretical analysis can all provide insight, connections, contexts and frames of reference that will inform your work. In many art schools, you'll find that theory informs practice, a fusion that aims to empower students and encourage critical self-awareness without stifling intuitive creativity. Students of illustration should aim to be self-motivated and self-reliant, proactive and resourceful and actively engaged with visual global culture, ethically, critically and creatively.

Finding your own path, personal agenda and subject matter will grow from your engaging with the world and drawing on your experiences. Observe all aspects of culture and capture unexpected situations and emotions by learning to look, think, draw, edit, interpret and tell stories in your own remarkable and unique way. Your image-making process should be as personal and original as your handwriting.

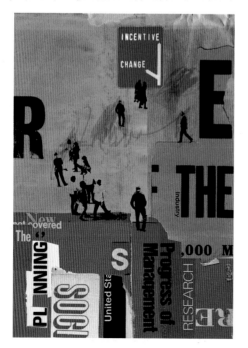

Title
Editorial magazine example (left) and book-publishing example (right)
Illustrator
Michelle Thompson
Description
Collage images

'I think the gap between design and illustration is closing. Illustrators are being given more open briefs from designers. There seems to be a better understanding of illustration and its uses.'
Michelle Thompson

Immersing yourself in all aspects of this evolving discipline will lead to the development of your own distinctive visual language and preferred working method(s). It will also help to shape an intellectual curiosity that will be combined with an appreciation of other related disciplines, methodologies and strategies. Through an open-minded and self-reflexive approach to learning you can contextualise your personal concerns and goals.

You should aim to initiate dialogues, transcend discipline-centred boundaries and interrogate the roles, status and power relationships of the global creative industries. An important aspect of study is to decode the process of image interpretation by engaging multidisciplinary methodologies. Through a holistic and critical analysis of a wide range of theoretical frameworks and divergent narratives, try and find synergies, commonalities, contradictions and disconnections, to initiate and develop arguments, compare theories and test analytical tools.

Illustration is a hybridised and multifaceted activity, and by embedding cultural pluralism, illustrators can challenge preconceptions, test boundaries and subvert the hierarchies and conventions of art and design education and practice.

Title
Rubicks EP
Illustrator
Brett Ryder
Description
CD packaging

BUMO

Title
BUMO
Illustrator
Andy Potts
Description
Personal illustration
work (digital print)

Mapping connections and directions

Adopting an interdisciplinary and perspectival approach will help you develop critical insights and awareness. These deep learning strategies provide a breadth and depth of practice. It's all about engaging and connecting with the world, being observant, sceptical and culturally literate; reading books, blogs, websites and gathering as many sources of primary and secondary research as is possible.

To get you started, read, compare and reflect on the theories and methods of analysis of philosophers, social theorists, linguists, critics and writers such as:

Georg Wilhelm Friedrich Hegel	Karl Marx	Luce Irigaray	Herbert Marcuse
Marshall McLuhan	Jacques Derrida	Walter Benjamin	William Gibson
Jean-François Lyotard	Ferdinand de Saussure	Gilles Deleuze	Edward Tufte
John Berger	Charles Peirce	Jacques Lacan	Ellen Lupton
Michel Foucault	Umberto Eco	EH Gombrich	Kalle Lasn
Jean Baudrillard	Dick Hebdige	Søren Kierkegaard	Paul Klee
Guy Debord	Victor Papanek	Friedrich Nietzsche	Albert Einstein
Roland Barthes	JA Walker	Martin Heidegger	Richard Buckminster Fuller
Immanuel Kant	Noam Chomsky	Albert Camus	Naomi Klein
	Julia Kristeva	Ludwig Wittgenstein	Victor Margolin
		CG Jung	

Then complement your explorations of critical discourse theory by analysing the rich and diverse histories of illustration and its relationship to changes in the means of production and consumption, developing technologies and increasingly diverse audiences.

Exploring a wide range of alternative methodologies, including the study of signs, semiotics, semantics, language, linguistics, rhetoric and the dialectic of words and images, will also enhance your learning experience.

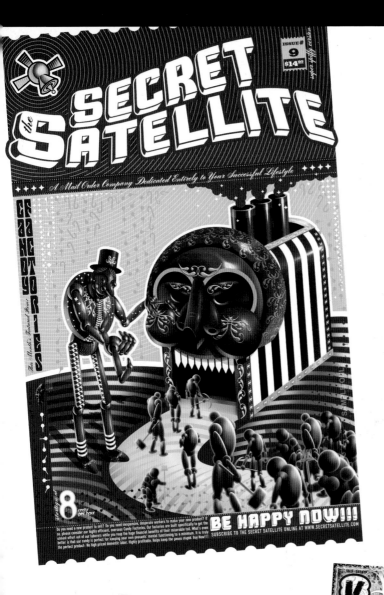

Title
Secret Satellite
Illustrator
Kristian Olson
Description
Posters created using
existing letterforms
embellished with a
personal touch

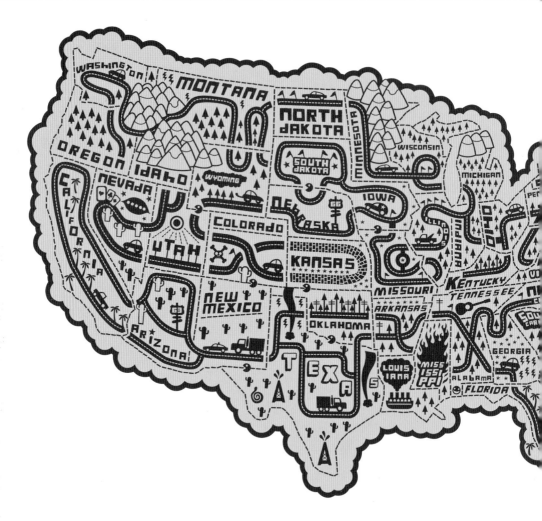

'I worked as a graphic designer before working in illustration –
having an understanding of layout, design and type skills is invaluable.
I find laying type out on a page has illustrative qualities, you have
to see which way the letters and paragraphs flow best and have
an understanding of visual hierarchy…. The lines between design
and illustration are increasingly blurred. At Camberwell I studied
graphic design, but my tutor was an illustrator. I think it shows
that illustration and design all come under the umbrella of visual
art and you have the choice to solve a brief through whichever
visual aid works for that project.'
Serge Seidlitz

Title:
USA Roadmap (left)
and Teen Wolf (this
page)
Illustrator
Serge Seidlitz

An interdisciplinary ethos

There is a huge range of key contemporary critical debates, theories, critiques and ideas that can also enhance and inform your study of illustration. Some of these include, but are not limited to:

a personal and professional ethos

ethics and social responsibility

authorship

communication theories

film theory

literary theory

the history of art and design

education

theatre structures

entrepreneurship

collaboration and teamwork skills

mass communication

demographic trends

micro politics

intellectual copyright and capital

business studies

quantum physics

chaos theory

perceptual psychology

sociology

media studies

political philosophy

neo-liberal capitalism and the free market economy

beliefs and religions

moral philosophies

Confucianism

Aristotelianism

Buddhism

Taoism

Marxism

anthropology

pragmatism

semiology

transcendentalism

phenomenology

science

the history of ideas

existentialism

aesthetics

epistemological models and artistic grammars

Epicureanism

formalism

theoretical structures from analytical philosophy

Hegelian idealism

cognitive sciences (from Descartes to gestalt theory)

intelligence theory

situationism

psychogeography and simulacrum

poetics

phenomenological hermeneutics and the interpretation of texts and human behaviour

Habermasianism

usability

dialectical materialism

modernism

the avant-garde

post-structuralism

intertextuality

deconstruction

postmodernism

the ideological functions of artefacts

multiculturalism

the politics of the body

feminism

the globalisation of culture

alienation and entertainment

celebrity culture

branding and the fetishism of products

virtual communities

gesamstkunstwerk

interpretation and misinterpretation

spectatorship

the ethics of difference

cultural identity

desire and advertising

lifestyle and values marketing

cross-cultural communication

representation, production and consumption

homogeneous consumer culture

rapid technological change and the compression of distance, space and time

the convergence of media surveillance

game culture

social networking sites

simulation

artificial intelligence

an awareness of eco design and the principles of environmental sustainability

Neasden Control Centre

Pictured opposite are some digital stills taken from Neasden Control Centre's eclectic showreel of low-tech layered and spliced motion graphic work. The visuals are produced through free-form association of images collected in sketchbooks and scrapbooks.

Viewed from the top left to bottom right:
Change the World/MTV UK: Steve Smith/Neasden Control Centre
Island Records/Identity: Steve Smith & Marcus Diamond/Neasden Control Centre (art directed by Surround)
The Interview/ICA/The Show: Steve Smith/Neasden Control Centre

A subjective history of illustration

There are many and varied published histories of art, graphic design and book illustration, but as yet there are none of illustration as a discipline in its own right. It is an elusive subject; perhaps the whole history of the human race itself is, in part, based on the visual languages of illustration. This leaves us free to write our own history and to plunder the arts, sciences and philosophies in order to compile our own eclectic and personal canons of influence.

Every student of illustration needs to seek out the rich history and development of both the discipline and profession of the subject. You should research other related disciplines, media and genres such as architecture, painting, graphic design, film, theatre, fashion, interior design, textiles, product design, sculpture, ceramics, dance, street art, computer games, animation, interactive media, photography, folk and outsider art and comic art.

Traditional, linear chronologies of the history of illustration, graphic design or commercial art usually emphasise styles, genres and the achievements of its heroes. But canons of influential individuals within the subject's history require expansion and should be underpinned with cultural pluralism, and the multiple meanings of illustrations should be deciphered and decoded. The complexities, functions, values and beliefs associated with images and artefacts should be investigated for their social, theoretical, historical, cultural, ideological, technological, economic and political contexts.

On pages 30–33 you'll find a subjective chart of key individuals, events, inventions, tools and movements, which blur discipline boundaries and suggest a diverse kaleidoscopic history. This chart should be used as a starting point for further discourse and exploration. Devise your own chart, one that reflects your own unique and distinctive professional ethos, working methodologies and personal visual language.

Title
Fiona Apple Portrait (opposite)
Illustrator
Olaf Hajek
Description
Surrealism-informed portrait for Rolling Stone magazine

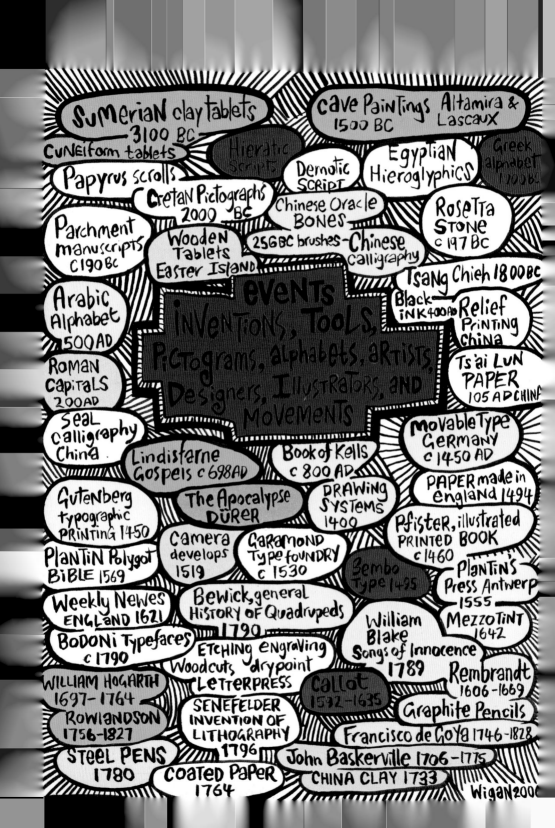

Rubens Title Pages Osidio Bredana 1626

COLOUR ENGRAVING 1719

FAT FACE TYPE 1803

encyclopédie 1751–1772 Diderot and d'Alembert

colour Ukiyo-e Prints Harunobu 1765

Paul Sandby 725–1809

1800 CAST-IRON PRESS

IVORY CARD 1820

STEAM-POWERED PRESS 1814

SANS-SERIF TYPE 1816

Delacroix illustrations for FAUST 1828

WOODTYPE POSTERS 1850's

Dayuerre & Talbot 1839 PHOTOGRAPHY

GEORGE CRUIKSHANK 1792–1878

Rotary lithographic Press 1846

Walter Crane

PHOTOLITHOGRAPHY NIEPCE c 1822

INDUSTRIAL REVOLUTION

Edward Lear

MONOTYPE machine 1887

ARTS AND CRAFTS MOVEMENT

Halftone Screens 1885

ART NOUVEAU

ART WORKERS GUILD 1884

Silkscreen Printing

CHromolithography

aquatint

Collotype

Linotype 1876

Wood engraving

4 colour PROCESS

Steel engraving

Photogravure

GUSTAVE DORE 1832–1883

WILLIAM MORRIS 1834–1896

BEARDSLEY 1872–1898

OWEN JONES

JULES CHÉRET

The Beggarstaff Brother

Hokusai

Kate Greenaway

Henri de Toulouse Lautrec

Punch

Grandville

Le Charivari

Tenniel

Kelmscott Press 1891

The Illustrated London News

Jugendstil

Samuel Palmer

GUSTAV KLIMT

Hiroshige

Wiener Werkstätte

Alphonse Mucha

T-A Steinlen

Peter Behrens

Arthur Rackham

John Hassell

eugène Grasset

1897 The forming of Vienna Secession

Theodore Lowe de Vinne

Plakatstil

Lucian Bernhard

Joseph Hoffmann

Maxfield Parrish

Ludwig Hohlwein

James Merrit Ives 1824–1895

Edgar Degas 1834–1917

Twigan 2006

PICASSO

CUBISM

A.M CASSANDRE 1901 – 1968

EXPRESSIONISM

ERIC GILL 1882 – 1940

MARCEL DUCHAMP

ART DECO

Edward McKnight Kauffer

Jean Carlu

FUTURISM

MARINETTI

H. HOCHE

DADA

MAN RAY

WILLIAM ADDISON DWIGGINS

KURT SCHWITTERS

GEORGE GROSZ

JOHN HEARTFIELD

MAYAKOVSKY

Lászlo Moholy-Nagy

CONSTRUCTIVISM

RODCHENKO

EL LISSITZKY

MODERNISM

PIET ZWART

BAUHAUS

HERBERT BAYER

DE STIJL

Jan Tschichold

ABRAM GAMES

BRODOVITCH 1950's

SURREALISM

TWEN magazine 1959

THE NEW TYPOGRAPHY

BEN SHAHN

ACRYLICS 1954

SAUL BASS

THE NEW YORK SCHOOL

ABSTRACT EXPRESSIONISM

THE INTERNATIONAL TYPOGRAPHIC STYLE

PARIS 1968

GRAPUS

PAUL RAND

LETRASET 1960

PUSH PIN STUDIOS

POP ART 1960's

CORPORATE IDENTITY

SAUL STEINBERG

CONCEPTUAL IMAGE MAKING

IKKO TANAKA

BRODY

Psychedelia

Tomi Ungerer

MILTON GLASER

FLUXUS

JACK KIRBY

RALPH STEADMAN

POST MODERNISM

PUNK 1976

TERRY JONES i-D

COLOUR XEROGRAPHY 1972

THE DIGITAL REVOLUTION

apple macintosh 1984

DESK TOP PUBLISHING

WORLDWIDE WEB

BRUCE MAU

TOMATO

DAVID CARSON

EMIGRE

CHRIS WARE

ED FELLA

STEVE BELL

Wigan 2006

Erik Spiekermann
Alan Fletcher
Herb Lubalin
April Greiman
RAW
Vaughn Oliver
Peter Saville
ZAP Comix
Tibor Kalman
Polish Posters
Wolfgang Weingart
Robert Crumb
Superflat
Barbara Kruger
ART and LANGUAGE
Kyle Cooper
Keith Haring
Lawrence Weiner
Edward RUSCHA
YOSHITOMO NARA
Jamie Reid
Alan Kitching
Raymond Pettibon
Fuse
JEAN-MICHEL BASQUIAT
Christopher Wool
Jenny Holzer
Guerrilla Girls
graffiti
Global POP
Juxtapoz
Paula Scher
WEB Design
Ian Hamilton Finlay
Barry McGee
Sue Coe
Manga
Geoff McFetridge
ZINES
Photo SHOP
Jeff Fisher
Art Chantry
Adbusters magazine
Gary Panter
Sara Fanelli
Marion Deuchars
Coop
Clayton Brothers
Plazm
House Industries
Barnbrook
Stefan Sagmeister
motion graphics
concrete POETRY
Handmade lettering
Tomoko Takahashi
FLASH
WIGAN 2006

Type play projects

As most illustrators know, project briefs are written to be subverted. Take the following suggestions and sample, remix and rewrite according to the needs of different types of audience. The emphasis should be on experimentation, so be open to chance, risk and mistakes and think laterally.

First, read the project brief and then make lists of anything that comes into your mind. Then deploy primary and secondary research, ask questions and place your project in a range of contexts. Ideas and visual metaphors will emerge from your research. The more ideas you generate, the more chance you have of creating something that is effective and original.

With each project synthesise elements, develop new techniques, employ your imagination and ask yourself if the work is appropriate. If not, refine your visual language, generate and elaborate on your visual concepts and manipulate aspects such as form, tone, line, colour, movement, positive and negative space, composition, weight, density, texture and scale. Demonstrate awareness of:

the proactive role of the reader/user/audience	ambition
working methodologies	experimentation
breadth and depth of research	innovation
thoroughness	the defining, solving and setting of problems
attention to detail	allowing mistakes
intellectual curiosity	self-critical awareness
persistence	autonomy and confidence
professionalism	a personal approach and direction
play	resourcefulness
point of view	awareness of ethical implications
technical accomplishment	responsibility
comprehension of brief	time management

Finally, relate your work to that of others and comment on and evaluate your work critically. Remember to have fun!

'All kinds of letters that exist, and that includes type letters and amateur letters, have their own intrinsic moods and meanings. Lettering is, for all its perfectionism, an expressionistic art.'
Ben Shahn

The Elucidators

Project 1: Urban poetry

Choose a poem that evokes and celebrates the countryside or nature. Edit a few lines from the poem, enlarge and manipulate the words, use letterforms that you feel are appropriate and place the words in a city street, then record your installation with photographs or video.

Research and inspiration
Ian Hamilton Finlay, Graffiti Research Lab, pattern and concrete poetry.

Project 2: There was an old lady from

Write and illustrate six of your own limericks.

Research and inspiration
Edward Lear's *A Book of Nonsense* (1845).

Project 3: What does it say?

Choose a word. Now design a letterform for the word that is as clear and legible as possible. Frame the word and manipulate it within the frame. How does the reader's perception of the word change? What emotions does cropping the word suggest? Represent the word through six stages until it becomes completely illegible. Split, degrade or distress the letterform. At what point does it become illegible?

Research and inspiration
Futurism, Dadaism, David Carson, Tomato, early issues of *i-D*, *8vo*, *ATTIK*, Stefan Sagmeister, Neville Brody, Jonathan Barnbrook, Eduardo Recife.

Project 4: That's rubbish

Design an alphabet from refuse or found objects. Digitally photograph or scan the objects and import them into digital font design software. Create your own 'Rubbish' font.

Research and inspiration
Filippo Tommasso Marinetti, Paul Elliman's Typotheque, Kurt Schwitters.

Project 5: Sign container

Create a narrative and design an appropriate container for it. Control the way the user accesses the narrative (for example, using navigational devices or layers).

Research and inspiration
Marcel Duchamp, Joseph Cornell, kinetic and book art.

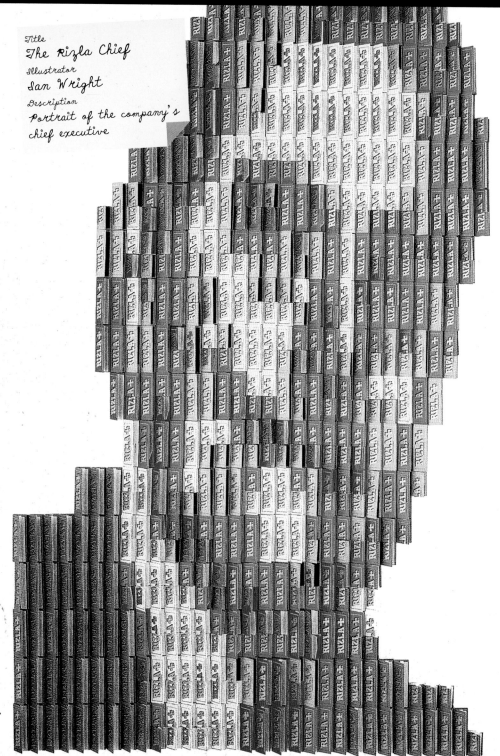

Title
The Rizla Chief

Illustrator
Ian Wright

Description
Portrait of the company's chief executive

The Oxford English Dictionary informs us that an illustrator is *'a person who draws or creates pictures for magazines, books, advertising, etc.'*, and that the origin of the word is late Middle English: *'from illumination, to shed light on; spiritual or intellectual enlightenment, from the Latin illustratio(n) and from the verb illustrare'*.

Illustrators shed light on a huge range of subject matter. They elucidate, clarify, decorate and communicate. The subject has a long and rich history, dating back to prehistoric cave paintings and covering media such as early picture writing, hieroglyphics, early codices, illuminated manuscripts, chapbooks, broadsides, posters, periodicals, postage stamps, comics and websites. Similarly, illustration is embedded in the development of communication technologies from clay tablets and scrolls to the printing press, film, television and the internet.

Much of the history of art is also the history of illustration. Traditionally many artists were commissioned to produce work for clients in specific formats and contexts, and representational pictorial art was closely linked to literature and the interpretation of religious texts, myths, legends, histories and important events. Then, as now, the illustrator interpreted and amplified ideas, messages and texts by transforming them into visual images, which either communicated by themselves or accompanied letterforms in a composition.

This chapter will:

explore a range of approaches that the illustrator can take to amplifying text,

introduce the concept of authorship in illustration,

review the area of self-initiated projects and book works,

provide a number of introductory sequential narrative projects.

The Rizla Chief (left)

Opposite is an image created by illustrator Ian Wright, who first gained recognition in the 1980s for his innovative portraits of musicians that interpreted his subject matter with unusual materials and processes. He now creates large-scale modular installations that make use of materials such as cassette tapes, badges, paper cups, drawing pins and salt. Wright's distinctive, consistent and prolific output continues with projects for Playlounge, Howies, The Design Council and The British Museum.

Amplifying the text

In order to successfully marry text and image and to visually extend, explain and enhance text, whilst keeping the authorial voice intact, the illustrator requires a passion for words. Intellectual curiosity, visual intelligence and cultural breadth (fuelled by reading a wide variety of genres of literature) are required.

Both reading and intensive practice in personal and expressive writing enables the illustrator to explore the construction of meaning and the interface between writer, artist and reader. Intensive and sustained engagement in the process of creative writing (such as poetry, fiction and prose for various audiences) enables the illustrator to analyse linguistic principles and solutions such as the argumentative, expository and rhetorical.

Orly Orbach

The work opposite is by London-based illustrator Orly Orbach. Orly studied at the University of Brighton and London's Royal College of Art, in the UK. She is interested in theatre and performance and has collaborated with actors, composers and performance artists. Commissions have included an installation at the Hayward Gallery, London, a film made with composer Lena Langer and a multi-sensory installation at the Trinity Buoy Wharf. In 2006, she won the Association of Illustrators gold award for design and new media with her *Burnt Book Box* project. Orbach exhibits her work in fine art galleries and illustrates for a number of publications including *LE GUN* and *Ambit*. For Orbach, illustration is a way of thinking and good illustration is all about interpretation. She seeks to make connections between the given text and her own personal interests and obsessions.

Orbach's approach to making the text personal and relevant often involves abandoning the original copy and researching other sources. This often means that her final illustration will reference these other sources. She states that 'the problem with language is it is referential to begin with. I think that by treating the text as image, and creating text using the same creative process you use to make pictures, you can bring the text back to life, and make it have a real presence again.'

Interpretation

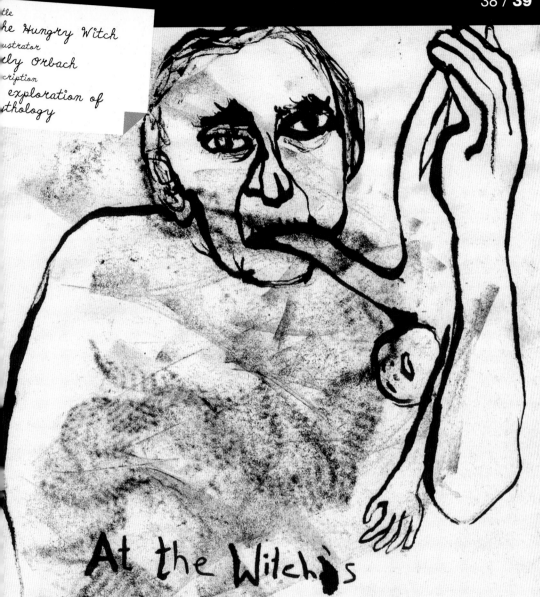

Title
The Hungry Witch
Illustrator
...ly Orbach
Description
...exploration of
...thology

At the Witch's
Trial, they asked her:
"Why did you eat your own grands
evil witch?
And she wept, and she said:
"I didn't mean to. I just wanted to kiss h
but he fell right in

Zoe Taylor

Illustrator Zoe Taylor graduated from London's Camberwell College of Arts before completing the MA programme in Communication Art and Design at The Royal College of Art. Zoe finds inspiration in folk tales, the films of David Lynch, literature, art and music, and is currently editor and founder of *Rag and Bone*, a magazine of folk culture and outsider art, which features artists such as Billy Childish, Clare Rojas, Fergus Hall, Rob Ryan and Espers. The magazine celebrates folk culture's enduring role as a source of creative inspiration and features new creative possibilities for folk imagery from around the world. The images featured on these pages were part of a sequential image-making project produced during her time at Camberwell.

Title
Le Chat noir
Illustrator
Zoe Taylor
Description
Pencil on newsprint monoprints

Pictured are Taylor's accompanying illustrations for *Le Chat Noir* (The Black Cat), a story found in Marian Roalfe Cox's *Cinderella*, which employ pencils, newsprint and monoprint techniques. Cox's book contains many curious and archaic versions of the Cinderella story from different cultures. Zoe was attracted to the text by its fragmentary and ambivalent nature and the twists and jolts of the story, which reflect the shifting nature of oral tradition. She has chosen to reference different periods of cultural history in her illustrations and avoid a Freudian interpretation of the folk tale. The skeletal format of the text, which concentrates on key events in each story, has enabled Zoe to create her own unique personal visual interpretation.

Author/illustrator

There is a long tradition of illustrators working as authors; inventing their own imaginary worlds, exploring them through writing and drawing and sometimes self-publishing their projects. These long-term personal projects are often sequential narratives and may take the form of children's books, graphic novels, comic books, limited-edition book works, animations, interactive media or visual essays.

Digital technology has empowered the illustrator as 'creator', providing greater control and ever more opportunities for expression. As well as narrative projects, illustrators can also self-initiate all kinds of promotional merchandise including badges, rubber stamps, digital and silk-screen prints, stickers, ceramics, wallpaper, tea towels, cards, textiles and T-shirts. These products are sold via shops, galleries or websites, providing a source of income and possibly leading to commissions by new or existing clients. Illustrators often use time set aside for personal projects to develop new techniques, experiment, take risks and refine their personal visual language. However, this entrepreneurial approach is not for everyone and some illustrators prefer to collaborate with other specialists, acquiring advice and feedback while concentrating on producing effective and appropriate images in response to the ideas of others.

The authorial approach certainly requires an expanded skill set and sees illustrators multitasking: employing the written word as well as facing the challenge of editing, designing and dealing with production and distribution issues. Successful author/illustrators understand that it's not just a matter of orchestrating a wide variety of processes, you must also have something to say. Influential visual storytellers whose work engages with content in intelligent, emotive, alluring and meaningful ways include Frans Masereel, Edward Gorey, Robert Crumb, Jeff Fisher, Tom Gauld, Andrej Klimowski, Sara Fanelli, Henrik Drescher, Maurice Sendak, Ralph Steadman, Glen Baxter, David Shrigley, Paul Davis, Marjane Satrapi, Chris Ware, Mark Beyer, Julie Doucet, Sue Coe, Daniel Clowes, Martin Tom Dieck and Joe Sacco.

Peter Arkle

New York-based illustrator Peter Arkle freelances for a variety of editorial and advertising clients. He illustrates a regular column, 'The Stalker', for *Print* magazine and also self publishes his own newspaper, *Peter Arkle News*, which has featured his hand-rendered drawings and text since 1993. The paper, which he mails to a growing number of subscribers, tells stories of Peter's everyday life. His work incorporates both text and image because, in his own words, 'I love jumping between the two things. Text and illustration are a great duo. I really hate when I hear art directors express a tired old convention that only bad illustrations contain words.'

Interpretation

A GUILTY
CONCIENCE
NEEDS NO
ACCUSER

BOUND
BY CON
DITION

adrianjohnson

IF YOU'RE
HAPPY AND
YOU KNOW
IT SLAP YOUR
FRIENDS.

Title
If you're happy and
you know it...
Illustrator
Adrian Johnson
Description
Proverbs used to
create new images

The author/illustrator requires a great deal of confidence and a high level of technical accomplishment built through self-determination, resourcefulness, passion and ambition. A strong work ethic is essential. This area of illustration is all about finding and following your own voice, personal critical concerns and point of view. AOI portfolio consultant Fig Taylor has worked as an illustrator's agent with a specialist interest in publishing. She lectures at illustration courses throughout the UK and thinks that within the field of children's books, publishers tend to look kindly on author/illustrators, but warns that 'if an illustrator is intending to take this path it is vital…that they understand the market they are attempting to break into'.

The internet is creating new markets for DIY projects. This allows illustrators to be autonomous and independent while challenging the existing status quo and traditional working parameters and conventions. However, in order to make a living from working in an author/illustrator capacity there must be an awareness of the importance of adhering to deadlines, self-promotion, and researching your target audience and market's needs. It is also essential to be aware of how your artwork will be reproduced and how different printing processes or on-screen applications will affect the quality of your imagery. Taking ethical and professional responsibility for the impact of your work on society, the environment and on the profession of illustration is another key concern.

Adrian Johnson

The work featured here is by author/illustrator Adrian Johnson. He uses a subtle colour palette and creates stylised characters with a witty retro feel. Johnson has produced a number of children's books such as *What! Cried Granny* as well as editorial, advertising and animation commissions for the likes of Orange, The Design Council (UK), Virgin and British Airways. Johnson is also a founder member of the UK-based illustration collective Black Convoy. Since its establishment in 2004, Black Convoy have collaborated on animations for onedotzero at the Hayward Gallery and exhibitions at east London's Seventeen gallery.

The visual journalist

For the illustrator, humanity and the world are our subject matter; all the stories and drama you could wish for are taking place right now in front of your eyes – all you need is a pen or pencil, a notebook and your mind. Pictorial journalism has a long history evident in the social commentary of artists as diverse as Jacques Callot, William Hogarth, Thomas Rowlandson, James Gillray, Toulouse Lautrec, George Grosz, Käthe Kollwitz, Eric Ravilious, Edward Ardizzone and Ben Shahn.

Historically, on-the-spot reportage images for newspapers and periodicals were produced by illustrators known as special or correspondent artists. Periodicals such as *The Illustrated London News*, *Paris L'Illustration*, *Der Sturm*, *Simplicissimus* and the *London Daily Graphic* featured the drawings of leading social reporters such as Paul Gavarni, Paul Renouard, Jules Pascin, Ernst Ludwig Kirchner and Oskar Kokoschka.

Despite the arrival of photography, the reportage tradition and the need to record real-life events has persisted and evolved. Exemplars of this illustrative style include Feliks Topolski's incisive illustrations for *The Listener*, Saul Steinberg for *The New Yorker*, Ralph Steadman's work for *Rolling Stone*, travelling artist Paul Hogarth's location drawings for magazines such as *Fortune*, Ronald Searle's visceral and moving prison camp drawings in *To the Kwai and Back: War Drawings 1939–1945*, and the work of Robert Weaver, Paul Cox, Posy Simmonds, Paul Davis and Olivier Kugler. Kugler recently created double-page spread reportage drawings for the *Guardian* newspaper, capturing likeness and atmosphere with his observational drawing then adding text as another layer of information to accompanying his images. He interviews the people that he draws and describes this as 'having the person I portray talking in their own voice, I guess I am more of a documenter [sic] than an author'.

Paul Hogarth

Students interested in following in the tradition of the pictorial journalist can discover fascinating insights and inspiration from the career of Royal Academician Paul Hogarth (1907–2002), who was described in the *New Statesman* as 'Britain's best descriptive graphic artist'. Hogarth cited Degas, Sir John Millais, Madox Brown and Arthur Boyd Houghton as influences on his work.

Recognised for his excellent draughtsmanship, Hogarth travelled around the world recording people, landscapes and buildings and capturing mood and atmosphere with pencil, conté crayon and watercolour.

Hogarth's compelling illustrations have appeared in numerous newspapers, books and magazines.

THE FRUIT & VEG GUY
OR ISON OF A MARKET TRADER

ONE VERY EARLY AND COLD SATURDAY MORNING ON BETHNAL GREEN ROAD...

① I'M 66 YEARS OLD. I'VE GOT MY STALL HERE FOR THE LAST 40 YEARS. BEFORE THAT I WAS WORKING TEN YEARS FOR MY FATHER AT HIS STALL IN BRICK LANE - BANGLATOWN, THEY CALL IT NOW. MY DAD, HE WAS HARD BUT HE WAS FAIR. BUT HE WASN'T FAIR SOMETIMES. HE WAS GIVING A STRANGER - THE OTHER BOY WHO WORKED FOR HIM - THREE QUID ON A SUNDAY AND I WORKED FOR 50 P. HE USED ME BUT HE LEARNED ME MY TRADE.

④ THE SUPER MARKETS

HAVE THEIR LITTLE BATTLES BETWEEN EACH OTHER, BUT THEY ARE KILLING US!

THEY ARE DOING EVERYTHING NOW AT TESCO, CAR INSURANCE, HOME INSURANCE, PET INSURANCE, EVERYTHING.

THE SUPERMARKETS THEY ARE SO GREEDY. THEY ARE GONNA FINISH IT UP. THEY'LL BE THE GOVERNORS. THE FRUIT AND VEG AT MY STALL IS CHEAPER THAN IN THE SUPERMARKET.

BUT THE WOMEN DON'T CARE! THEY GO INTO TESCOS AND SPEND EVERYTHING. THEY DON'T GIVE A SHIT.

PETER HERBERT

I'M RETIRING IN SEPTEMBER. I'LL PROBABLY GO ROUND THE BEND WHEN I DON'T KNOW WHAT TO DO WITH MYSELF. I'LL CREEP UP THE PUB AND HAVE A PINT I SUPPOSE.

② I'VE GOT MY STALL HERE FROM TUESDAY TO SATURDAY. IN THE MORNING I GET UP AT TWO O'CLOCK. THEN I DRIVE ME VAN DOWN TO LEYTONSTONE MARKET, WHERE I DO MY BUYING. I COME DOWN TO BETHNAL GREEN ABOUT SIX O'CLOCK AND GET MY STALL OUT. IT'S A BIG STALL, A HEAVY STALL, LIKE AN ELEPHANT. I GET IT OVER TO MY PITCH, PULL UP HERE AND HAVE A REST.

③ I'VE GOT TWO BROTHERS, JAMES AND JOHN. JOHN IS AN INSURANCE BROKER. JAMES IS THE HORROR WRITER. I READ ONE OF HIS BOOKS, THE RATS. I DON'T LIKE BOOKS, I LIKE VIDEO, I CAN'T READ BOOKS. I CAN'T DIGEST THEM. I'M NOT INTELLIGENT ANYWAY. MY BROTHER JAMES IS LIKE CLIFF RICHARD. HIS RECORDS, HE'S DONE THEM IN ALL DIFFERENT ... S, ALL OVER THE WORLD, LIKE MY BROTHER ... O - YOU CAN BUY HIS BOOKS IN GERMAN, ... ITALIAN.

Titles
Fruit & Veg Guy (top) and *Bingo*
Illustrator
Olivier Kugler
Description
Reportage images

... 'S ABOUT FIVE MINUTES. ... AIN SOMEONE TO CALL THE GAME. BUT IT TAKES A LOT, LOT LONGER TO BECOME A VERY, VERY GOOD CALLER. YOU NEED TO HAVE A GOOD, STRONG PERSONALITY,

BECAUSE THE CUSTOMERS NEED TO KNOW YOU'RE CONTROLLING THE GAME. IF YOU'RE NOT THEY'LL TRY AND TAKE YOU FOR A RIDE. THEY'LL TRY AND GET YOU TO GIVE THEM MONEY WHEN THEY SHOULDN'T HAVE MONEY.

③ ONE OF THE THINGS I DO, AND A LOT OF GOOD BINGO CALLERS DO, IS PLAGIARISE. IF YOU HEAR SOMEBODY CRACK A FUNNY JOKE AND YOU THINK THAT WILL WORK, THEN YOU NICK IT. A LOT OF THE STUFF YOU SEE ME DO ON STAGE I'VE NICKED FROM OTHER CALLERS.

BINGO HALL, BOGNOR REGIS 17 NOV 05

CAL LING

NUMBER 60
TOTAL PRIZE MONEY £ 45·00
NATIONAL GAME

THREE ON ITS OWN, NUMBER THREE!

① BEING A BINGO CALLER WAS MEANT TO BE A STOP-GAP, BUT THE THING IS, I LOVE IT!

I'M LIVING IN SIN WITH MY GIRLFRIEND. WE'RE BOTH STILL YOUNG. THE RELATIONSHIP IS GOOD.

AND I LOVE CALLING BINGO NUMBERS.

④ AT THE CHAMPIONSHIPS
YOU'RE JUDGED ON THREE DIFFERENT THINGS:
THE JUDGES WILL GIVE YOU AN INTERVIEW, ASKING QUESTIONS ABOUT THE BINGO INDUSTRY. THEN YOU GO ONSTAGE IN FRONT OF ABOUT 1,500 PEOPLE AND ENTERTAIN THEM FOR THREE MINUTES. AND THEN THERE'S THE ACTUAL CALLING.
THE ONLY THING I'M PRACTISING AT THE MOMENT IS MY THREE MINUTES OF ENTERTAINMENT. I'M GOING TO DO SOME KIND OF MIND-READING TRICK, I THINK. I WON'T DIVULGE ANY MORE BECAUSE I DON'T WANT TO SPOIL IT.

BRETT HYRJAK

At the present time, digital technology provides the illustrator with a multitude of new options, opportunities, methodologies and techniques. Tools such as mobile phones and digital cameras can be used to gather visual research and construct illustrations, but if one thing is going to set you apart then it must be the compulsion to draw.

If going out on location with a pencil and a sketchbook seems to be an unfashionable activity, I argue that this is precisely the reason to do it. Following trends in our media-saturated society only confirms that it is easier to copy than to think. Look, see and think. Observe the world, draw and inject your personal viewpoint. Your ideas, convictions, interests and imagination will lead you to find and tell visual stories. Discover inspiration and new thoughts and feelings by creating a dialogue with yourself.

Drawing is visual thinking. It enables you to communicate the emotions, drama and feelings inherent in the interaction of people, objects, animals, architecture, landscapes and locations. Experiment with a broad range of mark-making media techniques and materials and develop your own personal approach to drawing. Try to express emotions, elucidate ideas and capture the moment. In attempting to do this consider the following:

visual relationships	tone	perspective
atmosphere	composition	patterns
mood	metaphors	rhythms
proportion	analogy	movement
scale	abstraction	transitions
form	colour	subtracting or synthesising
space	lighting	elements
balance	contrast	
line	juxtaposition	

If your work demonstrates passion, impact, originality, integrity and creative prowess there will be people willing to publish it and, as mentioned on the previous pages, you could also publish it yourself.

'I like the term Visual Journalist, it suggests an engagement with society, a search for truth, exposing the unseen.'
Paul Bowman

Interpretation

Title
Untitled (massacre of
8,000 Muslim men and
boys by the forces of
Ratko Mladic)
Illustrator
Paul Bowman

Book art

'Mere vanity publishing', 'pure self-indulgence' or 'you can't make a living from this'! These are certainly some of the views that many in the communication design industry take on book art. However, with the constant blurring of definitions such as 'illustrator', 'artist' and 'designer', book art is becoming an inspirational focus point for students from many art and design disciplines.

Nowadays, book art reaches beyond the traditional ink and paper format, and incorporates a vast range of materials, techniques and methodologies. Challenging, multidisciplinary and experimental, the book art genre encompasses approaches from multiple to limited edition *livres d'artistes*, from small press handcrafted books to book-like works of art, and from tiny objects to huge installations. Those who have pioneered development in this field include William Morris, the Kelmscott Press, William Blake, Ambroise Vollard, the Futurists, Dadaists, Surrealists, Marcel Duchamp, Max Ernst, Sonia Delaunay, Jean Dubuffet, Fluxus, Ed Ruscha, Liliane Lijn, Dieter Roth, Sol LeWitt, Tom Philips and Rachel Whiteread.

Emma Rendel

Experimental book art can be an inspirational element in the curriculum for an illustration student. Many illustrators are now writing, illustrating, designing, publishing and distributing their own books via online exhibitions, galleries and shops. RCA graduate Emma Rendel has published a series of books such as *The Awkwardists*, *Deathgirl*, *Deathgirl's Birthday* and *Deathgirl's Diary*. Her thoughts encapsulate the feeling of creative freedom and control that is driving many illustrators to self publish:

'I don't think I would be happy only doing illustrations for others even though that is where you actually get paid. For me it gets interesting when I get to decide the pace of the story; it is a bit like directing a film, where should it be quick or slow, where should it be loud or quiet? When I write my own text I can choose to say things in the pictures instead of in words, and sometimes even take out the words if the pictures can say what's intended in a more effective way.'

Interpretation

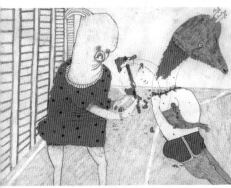

Dear diary.
Today I managed
to get the present
I know that it is
the best gift. Maybe
now he will fall in
love with me.

Title
Work from Deathgirl
(top) and Cowboy
(left)
Illustrator
Emma Rendel

I was as happy as I could be, but my guilty consciousness tore at my soul, and I lived in constant fear of being exposed as the dancing fraud I was. One night I took my fourteen children and fled. For five years we have been hiding from the alligators and the blood-thirsty cowboy-mobs under the Blackfriars Bridge. But my crime wont leave me in peace, there is not a day without tears or a night without nightmares.

Self-publishing

Exploring the book as a vehicle for personal creative expression allows illustrators to investigate and integrate:

form and function	**format**	**pacing**
content	paper	pagination
narrative	**engineering**	**sequence**
structure	text, image and object relationships	juxtaposition
texture		**time**

The illustrator's conceptual process of generating ideas, planning, creating visual experiences for the reader and manipulating space, meaning and time can be enhanced by physically making books. Personal themes explored in 'made' books range from responses to geographical locations, walks and journeys to autobiographical material and childhood memories. Formats amplify and extend themes through visual rhythm, variety and emphasis.

Traditional, pre-digital crafts, skills and techniques that can underpin such work include hand binding (such as Japanese stab binding, long stitch, cased, cloth, Coptic, in board and Chinese binding), and typesetting by hand (such as using wood type and raised metal type letterpress, or integrating type with printed images). Commercially obsolete technology is loaded with analogue mystique and artistic connotations for the illustrator.

Online publishing, moving image, installation, graphic design and performance are also presenting areas in which to explore, challenge and develop the concept of the book. There are a variety of approaches and definitions to this expanding time-based genre. Research, interrogate and analyse historical and contemporary contexts relating book works to their semantic, cultural, social and ideological functions. At the imaginative forefront of this activity in the UK are artists and online distributors such as Mark Pawson, Craig Atkinson's Café Royal, little paper planes and Concrete Hermit (whose work is featured opposite).

Other related 'making' activities can include papermaking, sculptural book forms, puppetry, accordion folds, codex forms, pamphlets, concertina folds and pop-up books.

Title
Selection of illustrated
postcard books from
concretehermit.com

Illustrators
From top row: Andrew
Jones, Andrew Rae, Ian
Stevenson and SKWAK

Katherina Manolessou

Illustrator Katherina Manolessou has created a number of limited edition books working with silk screen, linocut and letterpress printing. These personal projects have helped her to visually narrate stories and develop her illustration work. She finds taking charge of the whole process, from idea generation to bookbinding, both challenging and fulfilling. Manolessou states that 'skills in typography, design and layout are essential for an image-maker, enabling you to speak the designer/art director's language, create self-promotional material and engage in a wider variety of projects'. Manolessou also collaborates on book projects with illustrator and printmaker Otto Dettmer, a collaboration she describes as 'unique and inspiring, providing insight into another artist's working process and making me re-evaluate my own work as well'.

Title
Pages from a collaborative book project
Illustrators
Katherina Manolessou and Otto Dettmer

External objects have
a real effect on the brain.
The person who shuts
himself up between four walls
finishes up loosing the ability
to associate ideas and words.

Otto Dettmer

Otto Dettmer works in the editorial design, advertising and book publishing fields and he has also self-produced a large number of photocopied and screen- and inkjet-printed books. His visual narratives focus on mythologies in contemporary culture such as consumerism, the work ethic and self-destruction. He observes that 'in the commercial world, illustration is often exploited for its decorative value, or even to make a meaningless or deceptive message look good' and believes that 'illustrators can be authors; although people don't take images seriously it might be time to train people to read text image hybrids'.

Dettmer promotes his work through his website (www.ottoillustration.com), which features witty conceptual illustrations for clients such as the *Guardian*, *Le Monde* and *The Economist*. Self-published artworks are also available on the site.

Title

Diary of an Amateur
Photographer (top)
and Woman's World
(right and below)

Illustrator

Graham Rawle

Symbiotic associations

Words and images have symbiotic associations for image-makers who hand-render text as an integral part of their practice (as can be seen in the work of Olivier Kugler, Raymond Pettibon, David Shrigley and Paul Davis) and when writers' and artists' minds meet (for example, AA Milne and EH Shepard, Lewis Carroll and Sir John Tenniel, Roald Dahl and Quentin Blake, and Neil Gaiman and Dave McKean).

Graham Rawle

Graham Rawle's 'Lost Consonants' series has appeared in the *Guardian* newspaper for the last 15 years; he has also created a series of illustrations for the *Observer* and *Sunday Times* newspapers. Rawle's witty, idiosyncratic and diverse output includes 'Niff Actuals', which blurs definitions between high art and commercially produced merchandise. Niff Institute artists create editioned pieces such as a non-specific tape measure and an 'It's my World' globe. The latter features speculative geography and cartographical guesswork painted from memory and is not to be relied on for matters of international political strategy or used as a serious navigation tool!

Rawle has written and illustrated a number of books including *Diary of an Amateur Photographer*, *Wonder Book of Fun* and, most recently, *Woman's World*. Set in 1962, *Woman's World* is about a cross-dressing man who fashions his female persona (Norma) from the women's magazines that he relies on for advice. This funny, original and disturbing full-length novel took five years to make and is an objet d'art containing 40,000 fragments of text (cut from a variety of 1960s women's magazines), which have been carefully edited to tell Norma's subversive story. Although the book features constantly changing fonts and type sizes, Rawle worked hard to design a type grid to make all the text legible. A narrow column of text, limited to 200 words per page with the occasional large word and spot illustration, made an effective design solution.

For Rawle, the idea determines the form the piece will take and the narrative content and protagonist's character will influence the book's use of text and image: 'the most important thing for me is to ensure that the story works; if readers aren't asking what happens next, they won't turn to the next page, however pretty or interesting it might look'. On *Woman's World*, Rawle goes on to say that 'both visually and in terms of the content, the words he/she uses retain the essence of their original context. It's what I love about collage'.

The visual journalist > **Book art** > Narrative illustration projects

Narrative illustration projects

Project 1: A pictorial guide to street life

Illustrate and design a guidebook that enables the viewer to navigate, discover and interact with unusual and bizarre social or cultural aspects of urban street life.

Explore and resolve sequential, formal and functional concerns. Consider the hierarchy of text, image and meaning. Identify a specific target audience, inject your own personal point of view and tone of voice.

Research and inspiration
Alfred Wainwright's pictorial guidebooks to walking in the Lakeland Fells, psychogeography and situationism, GPS, archaeology, festivals, parades, rituals, viral marketing, consumption, hobbies, branding, intervention art, markets, virtual worlds, subcultures, hidden places, pub crawls, urban foxes, vandalism, utopias, buskers, treasure hunts, transport, urbanism, ley lines, tagging, mapping, reportage, gangs, architecture, surveillance, game culture, phenomenology, sociology, science fiction.

Project 2: Land of hope and glory

Discover or invent a narrative set during the reign of England's Queen Victoria. Evoke the atmosphere and style of the era and make use of reference material. Let the format and physical structure of your project follow its function. Consider time, pacing, emphasis, rhythm, pop-ups, rubber stamps, inserts, paper folding, letterpress, silk screen, found paper, old postcards and memorabilia.

Research and inspiration

The industrial revolution, the British Empire, expeditions, popular folk art, coronation mugs, scrapbooks, punch and judy shows, glass snowstorms, public houses, toy theatres, peep shows, advertising, decorated narrowboats, political cartoons, toby jugs, inn signs, music halls, bandstands, the circus, periodicals, seaside souvenirs, curiosities, freak shows, sailor tattoos, inventions, pin cushions, tobacco jars, door knockers, horse brasses.

Project 3: Think globally, act locally

Making use of recycled materials (such as recycled papers and environmentally friendly inks), construct an awareness campaign on the impact of greenhouse gas emissions on the world's climate. Select your target audience: this could be your fellow illustrators and designers or those who commission and mass-produce ephemeral graphic artefacts.

Avoid the obvious clichéd imagery and design associated with this subject. If necessary reintroduce it and give it a twist. Produce a visual essay that highlights the issues and actions needed to be taken, or a series of posters that seek to persuade people to take action.

Research and inspiration

Advertising, graphic agitation, propaganda and persuasive image-making, *When the Wind Blows* by Raymond Briggs, John Heartfield's photomontages, Les Graphistes Associes, Grapus, Amnesty International posters.

Project 4: Born to be wild

Devise and illustrate a thought-provoking, inventive and intelligent ambient media campaign to highlight the plight of endangered species. Consider 2-, 3-, or 4D approaches, woodcut, etching, engraving, lithography, watercolour, magnetic and conductive paints (to embed LED display electronics), mobile marketing, projections, architectural interventions, badges, stickers and GIF animations.

Research and inspiration

WWF, field sketchbooks, expeditions to botanical gardens, zoos, the countryside, ornithological illustrators (such as John James Audubon, Thomas Bewick, Edward Lear and George Edwards).

THE BIG BANG

OR HOW I LEARNED TO STOP WORRYING AND LOVE CREATIVE THAT GETS RESULTS

Title
Big Bang
Illustrator
Andy Smith (for
Tequila)
Description
Three-colour
promotional book

Within today's visual communication industry, disciplines and media are converging, creating new hybrids and, with these, a new generation of mutant illustrator is emerging. Amidst the visual flux and rhetoric, these illustrators are orchestrating both text and image to persuade, educate, intrigue, entertain and instruct.

New technological developments provide numerous opportunities for the use of radical methodologies and strategies to communicate messages, narratives and ideas for increasingly sophisticated clients, users and audiences. Areas such as branding, corporate identity, film, ambient media, websites, publishing and editorial all require the creation and conveying of subject matter or content.

The illustrator continues to provide strong ideas, personal vision, experimentation, imagination and the handmade mark. Digitisation has provided new tools and media delivery channels and has also contributed to the erosion of specialisms and strictly defined disciplines. As such, the illustrator has had to be flexible and able to adapt to new communication delivery platforms. Recent years have seen a re-evaluation of the merits of craft-based techniques and the integration of analogue, handcrafted and traditional media and processes and their digital counterparts.

This is fuelled in part by a reaction to a perhaps cynical, corporate, commodity- and brand-driven society and in part by the pace of technological change. Formulaic digital image-making and prosaic handcrafted illustration are now both being utilised by business to enhance mundane products and brands to make them appear 'cool', 'street' or 'fashionable'. No form of visual communication is value-free and for many of the do-it-yourself generation of independent illustrators, integrity, responsibility and ethics are also fundamental to their practice.

This chapter will:

> **explore** the functions, rationale and processes of contemporary commercial illustration practice,
> **introduce** editorial and conceptual illustration, persuasive and informative image-making, identity and text as image,
> **review** examples of contemporary commercial practice,
> **provide** critical insights from practitioners and conceptual letterform projects.

The Big Bang (left)

When asked on his thoughts on the schism between design and illustration, Andy Smith states: 'I think it used to be a very wide division – design and illustration is now taught more as one and not two separate disciplines. Both designers and illustrators now work on the same medium, the computer,

Editorial illustration

'Traditional' editorial illustration tends to cover work for lifestyle magazines, colour supplements, journals, in-house corporate magazines and regional or national newspapers. But contemporary editorial illustrators are commissioned to convey messages and clarify content in a wide range of contexts and for a variety of outlets.

One of these is book publishing, which encompasses packaging, book jackets, fiction, non-fiction, educational, technical, specialist or showcase books, graphic novels, comics, and children's books. Other forms of commissions for editorial illustrators include below-the-line company reports, brochures, point-of-sale material, retail signage, websites, corporate identity designs, logotypes and exhibition design.

Editorial commissions sometimes require a series of images to be produced in the form of a visual essay. However, it's more usual for single images that employ concepts and metaphors and provide an alternative view that summarises and conveys the underlying meaning behind the text, to be commissioned for this market.

Traditional editorial illustration commissions have always provided vital employment for illustrators. However, factors that have had a recent impact on illustrators working in this market include competition from the increasing use of photographic visuals and designer-made digital collages, the transition from print to the internet as a source of immediate news information and an increasing awareness of the environmental cost of mass-produced printed media.

Magazine and newspaper circulations may be falling (as they are now just one form of numerous communication channels), but they continue to provide publishing opportunities for the visual messages, ideas and commentaries of illustrators. The resurgence of interest (or so-called renaissance) in illustration in recent years has led to an increase in illustrated commissions in areas such as advertising, fashion promotion, animation, comics, web design and editorial work. Magazines, newspapers and websites are now frequently opting to commission illustrations instead of photographs, but illustrators are also utilising digital cameras and incorporating photography into their work, thereby merging the two disciplines.

'The worst thing that can be done is having the text say one thing and the image just repeating that. The image should comment on the text and vice versa. Then things become interesting.'
Jonas Bergstrand

Title
Døden en Bekymring
Illustrator
Jonas Bergstrand
Description
Retro-style design

DØDEN EN BEKYMRING

TORGNY LINDGREN & ERIC ÅKERLUND

KRIMINALROMAN SAMLEREN

Charlesworth & Cash Productions
Presents:

Title
Wolfram
Illustrator
John Charlesworth
Description:
Digitally enhanced
movie poster

INTRODUCING:

Wolfram©

....A Wolf In Freak's Clothing.

18

An applied art

Editorial work allows illustrators to gain recognition, develop experience of working with others and provides a platform from which to develop a unique visual vocabulary. This area of illustration is fast paced; deadlines are short and fees remain fairly low. However, seeing your work in print on a regular basis is rewarding and may lead to other commissions. Your relationships with your art director, picture editor and agent (if you have one), are paramount.

When undertaking editorial work, it is essential that your brief gives a clear deadline and indicates a budget for the licensing of your image or a cancellation or 'kill' fee if your work does not go to print. Other items that you should look out for in your brief include:

whether initial roughs, comprehensives, thumbnails and revisions are required information about the copy and subject matter	consideration of the target audience of the publication the likely reproduction process/method the resolution and file format that is required	whether you will be working digitally or scanning or digitally photographing handcrafted artwork its position within the publication and in relation to a double-page spread	whether the artwork will be produced in two, three or four colours (or in black and white) the format and size of the illustration

Briefs are varied; they can range from the creation of political cartoons and caricatures to fashion illustrations and beyond. An illustrator should respond to their brief through a personal process of brainstorming, idea development, research gathering, the use of reference or observational and imaginative drawing, pictorial wit, intuition, problem solving and, if there is time, reflection.

In editorial work, therefore, technical adroitness and sound working methods are essential. The visual elements utilised by illustrators and designers such as syntax, contrast, texture, scale, hierarchy, balance, colour, juxtaposition, line, tone, use of white space and framing can be manipulated to communicate effectively and illuminate, evoke, elucidate, clarify and extend the text.

Working within the constraints and parameters set by picture editors and art directors while retaining creative freedom enables the illustrator to exercise interpretation and apply intellectual enquiry and empathy to the subject matter. Through a combination of idiosyncratic personal vision and magic, editorial illustrators rapidly and instinctively interpret, comment and chronicle societal events and concerns.

Conceptual image-making

Conceptual illustrators have always drawn inspiration and appropriated philosophies, theories, processes and visual languages from literature, cinema and music. Numerous art movements (including Expressionism, Cubism, Dadaism, Surrealism, particularly the highly influential work of René Magritte, Art Brut, Abstract Expressionism, pop art, folk art, stylised realism, hyperrealism and global pop) have also proved to be a rich source of inspiration for illustrators.

Conceptual illustration first emerged in the USA during the 1950s and reflected the increasingly complex dilemmas and concerns affecting society at the time. It has since become a leading genre within illustration. The work of Saul Steinberg, Alan Cober, Milton Glaser, Seymour Chwast, Brad Holland, George Hardie, Jules Feiffer, Marshall Arisman, Anita Kunz, Phil Wrigglesworth and Paul Davis exemplifies the conceptual illustration tradition by combining strong, original and thought-provoking ideas with personal vision and imagination.

Title
We are moving (left) and London Illustrators' Gathering (right)
Illustrator
Nishant Choksi
Description
Limited edition prints

Visual strategies for conceptual illustrators combine a personal working methodology and technique with an original voice and ideas. Conceptual illustrators provide commentary, they look beyond any obvious or literal interpretation and often utilise humour, play and wit in their work. This can be achieved by incorporating:

visual puns	transformations	**addition**	pastiche
symbolism	**synecdoche**	subtraction	**homage**
visual metaphors	economy	**substitution**	typograms
similes	**metonyms**	personification	**trompe l'œil**
analogies	silhouettes	**coincidence**	abstraction
satire	**rebuses**	parody	**denotation**
distortion	clichés	**allegory**	connotation
extended metaphors	**twists**	incongruity	
	montage	**surprise**	

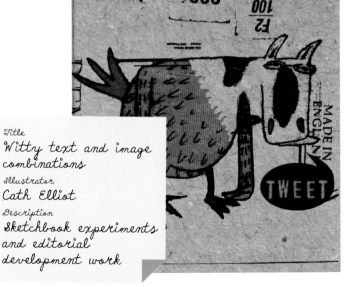

Title
Witty text and image combinations
Illustrator
Cath Elliot
Description
Sketchbook experiments and editorial development work

'I usually illustrate my own text, I get inspired by what's going on around me and I will pick up little snippets of conversation or interesting text I have read somewhere that finds its way into my illustrations.'
Cath Elliot

'*Most text-based work leaves a lot to be desired as it isn't very good and is based on jumping the bandwagon of what's trendy within the heady world of illustration. I see students not really trying to find their own voice – they see what's going on and think it cool to be part of some kind of 'movement' – there's so much stuff in portfolios that looks way too similar. It might look OK, but it has to be relevant and meaningful.*'
Paul Davis

Text, Images, Ideas and Messages

BullSystems

'I don't care and [I'm] not sure if there is a schism [between design and illustration] – it comes down to the individuals involved. Being at the arse-end of the creative process makes me mad sometimes.'
Paul Davis

Title
I can arrange a mortgage for you (right) and Pioneer (left)

Illustrator
Paul Davis

Description
A satirical corporate advert for the fictitious 'Bull Systems'

BullSystems

Persuasive image-making

One of the key functions of illustration and graphic design is to persuade audiences, readers and users to take action and to change their behaviour in some way. Images and text are employed and create a bombardment of global visual rhetoric that targets the desires, emotions, feelings and aspirations of specific audiences as it persuades, seduces, shocks, entertains and sells.

People define their identities and relationship to society by the products, services and brands they purchase and consume. Illustration has provided many iconic and persuasive images throughout the histories of propaganda, public relations and advertising and, it would appear that, illustration commissions for corporate multinational campaigns and brand identities are once more on the increase.

Illustration, with its connotations of authenticity and the emotive nature of the personal and decorative handmade mark, provides advertising with a seductive and effective tool and advertising is potentially a very lucrative sector for illustrators. However, contributing work to this area raises a number of ethical questions.

Advertising agencies commission above-the-line work such as billboard advertising and internet banner ads. In this line of work, fees are relatively high, deadlines short and negotiations with art directors, marketing departments and clients often involve a number of compromises and artwork revisions. Here, the collaboration between the art director and illustrator is the key to successful visual communication.

In this field, illustrators can often be perceived by art directors as too difficult to direct or too risky and unpredictable to collaborate with. However, art direction itself is no longer seen as the exclusive domain of the designer and some illustrators choose to assume both roles. Many though, prefer to concentrate on the image-making; for example, when asked for his thoughts on taking control of the whole process Andrew Rae commented that he was 'personally not interested in being a graphic designer or taking over that part of the job, I'm not meticulous or interested enough'.

Title
Come on in (top and bottom) and One Starry night (centre)
Illustrator
Andrew Rae
Description
Orange billboard posters and club flyer

Orange Broadband

the future's bright

Orange Broadband

the future's bright

'For an illustrator it's always really good to have skills in graphic design and typography. It makes your work much easier if you can think in layout terms when you compose your drawing. And sometimes the client wants hand drawn letterheads; then it's handy to have typographic skills.'
Dennis Eriksson

'Collect anything you find inspiring – cut out things from magazines, collect flyers, illustrations, interviews, ad campaigns and creative text or design. I have been doing this since college and have several A3 files rammed with things that have interested me and caught my eye.'
Matt Lee

Title
Florida Flames
(right)
Illustrator
Dennis Eriksson
Description
narrative illustration

Title
Thinking Head (below)
Illustrator
Matt Lee
Description
Conceptual illustration

Text, Images, Ideas and Messages

'Generally graphic designers
with no drawing ability are the
ones who believe the difference
between graphic design and
illustration is important.'
David Foldvari

Title
Urban street life
(below)
Illustrator
David Foldvari
Description
Edgy illustration

To instruct and inform

For the commercial artist, the key question is not just what media to work in but what client to work for and what effect will their work most likely have on the audience. Most illustrators are striving to create authentic, meaningful and intelligent visual communication in a responsible way. Many are choosing to combine their selected commercial work with not-for-profit and socially useful information design projects in order to instruct and inform.

The history of graphic art is full of examples of work by artists who said 'no' to the dominant prevailing ideology and to social injustices, such as: Francisco Goya, Honoré Daumier, James Gillray, Ben Shahn, John Heartfield, George Grosz, Käthe Kollwitz, Sue Coe, Jamie Reid and Joe Sacco, to name but a few.

As many image-makers amuse themselves with toys and trivia and by mimicking the latest trends, the planet's ecosystem is collapsing, worldwide human rights are being violated and the gap between the rich and the poor is widening. Historically, artists have held up a mirror (or in some cases a hammer) to the pressing issues affecting their age, and the major challenges facing the continued survival of the human race in this century, such as global citizenship, global justice, sustainability and sustainable development, are now being embedded in many art curricula throughout the world.

The illustration student seeking to influence people with their own personal language and subject matter may choose to express their own point of view on the world via official and unofficial channels. Illustration has often been employed to combine words and pictures that provoke action or plead, shock, influence, agitate, inform, instruct, warn and educate their audience.

Some illustrators choose to instruct and inform as part of a team in conjunction with specialists from other disciplines such as architects, interior designers and computer programmers, and contribute artwork to information design and educational projects. Such projects often require primary and secondary research and can encompass a wide range of areas such as:

instructional manuals	**illustration websites**	mapping	**information architecture**
exhibition design	maps	**navigation**	
encyclopedia	**graphs**	**hierarchy**	sociology
architecture	environmental	semiotics	**prototype design**
game design	graphics signage	**linguistics**	focus groups
children's books	**diagrams**	demographics	**testing and evaluation**
technical, botanical	pictograms	**ergonomics**	
and medical manuals	**psychology**	usability	logo design

Title
Accept and Proceed
Illustrator
Si Scott
Description
Logo design

'*Predominantly I like to work with found text, especially when it has undergone some form of degradation. Placing different words/letterforms together within an image can create confusion and also puzzling situations. For example a word in an image may not be followed by the image of that word. This then enters the realm of semiotics and signs.*'
Laura Scott

'*It's important to develop an awareness of what good design means to you. Thinking about the design of a page layout allows me to be far more considered when I compose an image. To ensure a picture doesn't lose its impact it needs to work well as a whole with all the other elements such as a title, blocks of type or even other pictures.*'
Salvatore Rubbino

Title
Juxtapositions (above)
Illustrator
Laura Scott
Description
Found text and mixed media collage.

Title
A Walk in New York
(right)
Illustrator
Salvatore Rubbino
Description
A book of sketches
from the Big Apple

'I use many different methods, from cutting out letters from old books, postcards and letters – just about anything that catches my eye.
To using the Mac to get the exact font I have in mind. Also I am still a huge fan of Letraset!'
Caroline Tomlinson

Title
'E' is for Elvis (top) and Who are you calling a Feminist (left)
Illustrator
Caroline Tomlinson
Description
Political collage illustrations

Persuasive image-making > **To instruct and inform** > Text as image and image as text

Text as image and image as text

Letterforms can be manipulated in many different ways depending on the mood or context to be conveyed. Artists who have made letterforms a central part of their practice include Christopher Wool, Barbara Kruger, Ed Ruscha, Cy Twombly, Robert Indiana, Louise Lawler and Peter Wegner.

Illustrators have also made letterforms an integral element in their visual vocabularies, examples of this include:

decorative initials of medieval scribes, **embellished letterforms**, fleurons and dingbats, **Jules Chéret's fluid art nouveau posters**, Saul Steinberg's incisive line, **Push Pin studio's cohesive designs**, Ben Shahn's idiosyncratic brush and pen alphabets and **Robert Crumb and Chris Ware's comic lettering.**

Title
When I want to kill myself...
Illustrator
Margie Schnibbe
Description
One of a series of autobiographical works

Examples of innovative use of witty text and image interplay include symbols, logos and trademarks, such as:

I Love New York (by Milton Glaser), **IBM and UPS (by Paul Rand)**, CBS (by William Golden), **AT&T (by Saul Bass)**, International Wool Secretariat logo (by Francesco Saroglia), **Nuclear Disarmament symbol (by Gerald Holtom)** and Solidarity Poland 80 (by Jerzy Janiszewski).

Residents of cities see an average of 5000 advertisements as day. Within this urban environment of officially sanctioned visual messages, artists continue to find innovative ways to communicate unofficial messages. Provocative interventions that present the pictorial syntax of writing in unexpected ways include the calligraphic graffiti of São Paolo by the pichaçäo graffitists (who utilise the entire city as their canvas).

Title
Burned all my bridges
Illustrator
Harry Malt
Description:
An example of Malt's incisive line and conceptual wit

'Texts come from a variety of diverse sources including the writings of Sigmund Freud and the scripted responses of phone-sex operators.'
Margie Schnibbe

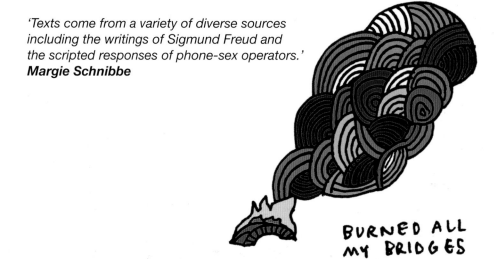

BURNED ALL MY BRIDGES

Title
Snowboards
Illustrator
John McFaul
Description
Illustrative type on
snowboards

'Generally when we use typography in
our illustrations it is hand-rendered.
So they are letterforms designed
specifically for the image.
Sometimes we may use an existing
font and alter it to get it looking
just how we want it. It's always nice
to feel like you have created every
part of your image and typography
is no exception.'
John McFaul

'I'm interested in handwritten fonts in illustration. Words are a powerful medium and combining typography into illustration is something I integrate a lot into my work. I have been influenced by words in illustration through reading comics, words always accompanied the images and this makes the words become a visual device in their own right.'
Serge Seidlitz

Title:
MTV Hits
Illustrator
Serge Seidlitz
Description
MTV indents and logos

Project 1: Sound poem

Cut up three completely different texts that are aimed at different audiences. Reassemble them and paste them into one poem. Generate six poems and accompany each with illustrations. Collate the poems into book form. Read or sing the poems to your peers, vary the pace, pitch and tone of your voice appropriately.

Research and inspiration
Kurt Schwitters, Filippo Tommaso Marinetti, Futurism, Dadaism, Brion Gysin, Patti Smith, William Burroughs, David Bowie, Albert-Birot, Jacques Derrida.

Project 2: Words as image and image as text

Employ wit and humour by integrating text and image into a single illustration. Select a short phrase and interpret it with handwritten or calligraphic techniques, or by manipulating a range of fonts.

Research and inspiration
Rebuses, coats of arms, puns, homage, ambiguity, conceptual art, Fluxus, pattern poetry, the calligrammes of Guillaume Apollinaire and John Cage's mesostics.

Project 3: Artist's signature

Create a series of letterforms that represent the name of a famous artist, illustrator or designer; choose a form that expresses the distinctive visual language of each artist. Do this for ten artists and experiment with a broad range of media.

Research and inspiration
Bas relief, embroidery, found objects, assemblage, stencils, felt tips, crayon, metal, laser cut, wood engraving, lithography, papier mâché, cut paper, string, dip pen, batik, Corel Painter, Adobe Illustrator, acrylic, oil paint, digital and traditional photography, wire, linocuts, spray paint, silk screen printing.

Project 4: 26 Letters

Create an illustrated alphabet of 26 letters. Construct each letter using a different media and technique.

Research and inspiration
Eric Gill, Alan Fletcher, George Hardie, Milton Glaser, Seymour Chwast, Nicklaus Troxler, Kyle Cooper, Lizzie Finn, Stefan Sagmeister, Jonathan Barnbrook, Paul Rand, *Fuse*, *Emigre*.

Project 5: Collage typography

Cut out black letters on white backgrounds and white letters on black backgrounds from different newspapers or magazines. Use these to create images that represent the following words: misery, aggression, harmony, fear, ecstasy, neurotic, satisfied, vertigo, melancholy, exuberant, isolation, love, claustrophobia. Explore perspective, weight, juxtaposition, form, shape, line, composition, rhythm, texture, movement and scale.

Research and inspiration
Cubist collage (for example, Braque, Picasso and Léger), Kurt Schwitters, Piet Zwart, HN Werkman, Wim Crouwel, Jan Bons, Vaughan Oliver, Jake Tilson, concrete poetry, Richard Hamilton, COBRA, Fluxus, Eduardo Paolozzi, Robert Rauschenberg, Peter Blake, John Heartfield.

Project 6: Three-dimensional text

Take a well-known phrase and turn it into a three-dimensional typographic object. Consider the way the phrase could exist in space and how it might be viewed. Is the work static or could it be moving (for example, a mobile)?

Research and inspiration
Kinetic sculpture, installation art, Braille and the work of Fiona Banner, Stefan Sagmeister, Eric Gill, Christopher Wool, Lawrence Weiner, Barbara Kruger, Edward Ruscha.

Project 7: Elucidate and amplify

Select one of the following texts to illustrate:

Short Stories (Anton Chekhov)

Dr Jekyll and Mr Hyde (Robert Louis Stevenson)

Poems of Love (John Donne)

Tales of Mystery and Imagination (Edgar Allan Poe)

Wuthering Heights (Emily Brontë)

Gulliver's Travels (Jonathan Swift)

The Goblin Market (Christina Rossetti)

On the Road (Jack Kerouac)

Working in your chosen media (for example, digital, handcrafted, photographic or any combination of these), create a series of illustrations. Generate concepts and roughs and then edit and clarify them. Focus on broad and structured research, drawing skills, your own personal voice and convictions, playfulness, process, observation, imagination, figuration, the use of reference, technique, props and models. Create the appropriate atmosphere and mood and empathise with the text.

Research and inspiration
Historical imagery and appropriate letterforms, Grandville, Aubrey Beardsley, Nigel Lambourne, Oskar Kokoschka, Max Beckmann, Franz Masereel, Charles Keeping.

Text as image and image as text > Letterform projects

every issue with
dual-format CD-ROM

www.computerarts.co.uk

computer
arts ®

Britain's biggest-selling creative magazine ◆ Mac & PC

Title
Computer Arts
magazine
Illustrator
Lawrence Zeegen
Description
Cover illustration

Over two thousand years old and still going strong, illustration is a constantly evolving and expanding art and craft. It is everywhere, an incredibly diverse and dynamic activity that is impossible to pigeonhole and engages with a myriad of complex channels of visual communication, delivery platforms and cultural contexts.

Practitioners nowadays are working within established constraints but continually challenge and transcend conventions and preconceptions of the subject. The illustrators featured in this chapter are at the forefront of the discipline's evolution by exploring and integrating traditional and new media, collaborating and working independently.

Practising in a wide range of contexts (for print, screen, set design, motion and interactivity), these illustrators are solving visual problems by communicating coherently, effectively and appropriately with unique personal working methodologies, visual languages and vocabularies. Combining practical skills, technical adroitness and draughtsmanship with intellectual engagement and critical thinking, they are making images to accompany, elucidate, illuminate and extend ideas, messages and texts with any media and technique.

Their approach is multifaceted. These illustrators are specialists, authors, critics, problem solvers, journalists, entrepreneurs, community artists, initiators and commentators who are all adhering to deadlines and making a living from their art. These artists are engaging with new technological possibilities and are critically and imaginatively aware of ethical and professional responsibilities, content context and their work's users and audiences.

This chapter will:

explore diverse individual and collaborative working methodologies in a range of contexts,
introduce a number of media and genres including posters, magazines, book jackets, installation and moving text and image,
review a range of historical and contemporary visual solutions,
provide critical insights and commentary from leading practitioners and introductory visual impact illustration projects and exercises.

Computer Arts magazine (left)

This cover design illustration was created for *Computer Arts* magazine by Lawrence Zeegen. The magazine reviews the latest computer hardware and software and features tips, tricks and tutorials for web design, typography, 3D animation, motion graphics and illustration.

Poster design

Posterists are innovators in the creative integration of text and image. From the papyrus posters of ancient Egypt to those commonly seen today, the role of the poster has always been to grab attention with its words and pictures and communicate directly with the viewer.

Posters inform, educate, appeal, protest and persuade with visual impact. Since the time of ancient Rome, a significant function of illustrated posters has been to encourage the consumption of products. Advertising is now a pervasive commercial activity; each year billions are spent on it worldwide. Illustrators are employed to create engaging and branded forms of entertainment. Their artwork is commissioned to align with brand personalities and values and to persuade consumers to buy products. But posters can transcend this function to capture the spirit of their time and echo social concerns and economic, technological, cultural and political changes.

Historically, the design of posters has been informed by advances in technology and influenced by the modern art forms of the time. Contemporary poster design is indebted to the pioneer of the medium, Jules Chéret (1836–1933), and his colour lithographic posters for the Parisian cabarets, music halls and theatres of the 1860s. Since then, posters have become a highly popular and collectable form of public art and have also influenced an array of other art forms. From La Belle Epoque, to communist regime political posters; those for Bauhaus and De Stijl, to Hollywood movie posters, circus posters and London Underground posters; and from Polish posters and psychedelic posters to the contemporary limited edition rock posters of Urban Inks, the genre is huge.

Posters have come to be recognised as powerful and influential examples of commissioned art. See page 170 for a survey of innovative and influential posters.

Title
Walthamstow Festival
Illustrator
Adam Graff
Description
Promotional posters

LIPTON ICE TEA PROUDLY PRESENTS...

Title
Lipton Ice Tea
Illustrator
Spencer Wilson
Description
Promotional poster

Title
Promotional posters
for Beth Orten
(top left), Wild Tigers
(left), and St Etienne
(top right)
Illustrator
Michael Gillette

Title
Murri poster
Illustrator
Stephen Fowler
Description
Urban Folk
events poster
(circa 2001–2005)

MURRI

Vanishing
Breed
NEW Electric
High LIFE

natty Bo
calypso and ska

hear
boris karloff
reading fairytales

No
3

Steve Beresford
and his
toy guitars

James
and
Beatrices
creekdippin hour of
twang

David Dubwise

plays
Nyahbinghi
Records

NERVOUS STEPHENS
mechanical
music set

Title
The Illustrated
Ape covers
Illustrators
Various
Description
A selection of classic
issues (2001–2006)

From chapbooks to broadsides; the dissident press of the 1860s and 1960s to glossy fashion periodicals; from Sunday supplements, football fanzines and comics, art school journals to 1970s cut 'n' paste punk fanzines; from technical manuals, wildlife, auto, sport, travel, design, computer or music monthlies to microzines with handpainted covers, all magazines utilise their own distinctive integration of words and images. A magazine's unique brand identity is created through the orchestration of typefaces, colour, format, layout, grids and mastheads.

Magazines frequently utilise decorative, narrative and conceptual images supplied by illustrators and photographers. The names of major figures from the history of art and design are intrinsically linked to the magazines that published their work. Exemplars include: Honoré Daumier and Paul Gavarni (*Le Charivari*), Richard Doyle, John Tenniel and John Leech (*Punch*), Norman Rockwell (the *Saturday Evening Post*), Saul Steinberg, Charles Addams and George Price (the *New Yorker*), Feliks Topolski (the *Listener*), Ralph Steadman (*Rolling Stone*), Robert Weaver (*Life*, *Sports Illustrated* and *Fortune*), Eric Fraser, Ronald Searle, George Hardie and Janet Woolley (the *Radio Times*), Harvey Kurtzman, Wally Wood and Will Elder (*Mad*), Milton Glaser, Seymour Chwast, Edward Sorel and Reynold Ruffins (*Push Pin Graphic*).

The illustration world often communicates through online and printed magazines such as www.illustrationmundo.com, the Japanese *Shift* and *Digmeout*, *IdN*, the AOI's *Varoom*, *Computer Arts* and *Computer Arts Projects*, *Eye Magazine*, *Artists and Illustrators Magazine*, *Illustration* (which is devoted to the history of American illustration) and *Illustration Magazine* (which is aimed at book collectors, fine-press printers and professional illustrators).

> '*I mainly commission out the work as I see it as a chance to give a lot of creative freedom to illustrators, which generally speaking doesn't happen too much in the commercial world... ultimately some of the best projects are described as collaborations between illustrators and designers.*'
> **Marcus Walters**

Poster design > Magazines > Installation and interventions

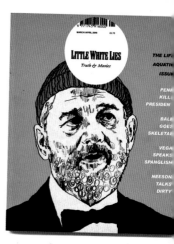

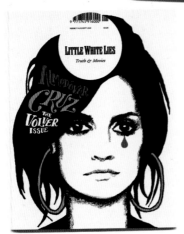

Title
Little White Lies

Illustrator
Paul Willoughby

Description
*A selection of iconic
covers from 2004–2006*

'Some illustrators do not make good
designers, they live in a world of dirty paint
brushes and obsessiveness; in this case it's
best to have a significant divide between the
intense subjectivity of the 'artist' and the
calculated objectivity of the designer.'
Paul Willoughby

LE GUN

LE GUN are: Bill Bragg, Alex Wright, Neal Fox, Matthew Appleton, Chris Bianchi and Rob Greene.

Bill studied illustration at Central Saint Martins, London. He is a freelance illustrator whose clients have included *Time* magazine, the *Independent* and the *New York Times*.

Alex has a degree in illustration and animation from Manchester Art School.

Neal has a degree in graphic design from Camberwell College of Arts, London. He is a freelance illustrator whose clients have included the *Guardian* and Random House. His most recent exhibition was 'The Aubergine Tongue' at The French House in London's Soho.

Matthew has degrees from Glasgow University and University College, London. After an illustrious career flipping burgers in Paris, he now works as designer for web, moving image and print. Past and present clients include Sony BMG, The Architecture Foundation, HP and the Royal College of Art.

Chris studied illustration at Middlesex University. He is a freelance illustrator and his clients have included Uniqlo and Tito in Japan. Known as 'Papa' to his friends, he also lectures in illustration at Norwich School of Art and Design.

Rob studied illustration at the University of West England in Bristol. He is a painter and illustrator and also one half of Soho's notorious double act The Rubbish Men a pair of Victorian punk revivalists who have been described as 'Beckett meets The Krankies'.

All six met on the communication art and design MA at the Royal College of Art in 2004, taught under Professor of Illustration, Andrzej Klimowski. It was here that the acclaimed graphic art periodical *LE GUN* was first conceived. The following insights are taken from a *LE GUN* team meeting:

What are your thoughts on telling stories in pictures, narrative illustration and text and image working in harmony?

Bill: A lot of our narratives are silent. It's difficult to tell a story with both pictures and words, you don't want to illustrate text too directly, you don't want to say too much.

Chris: My stories are like silent movies.

Bill: But then again, I remember saying the same thing to Tony Fish and he said 'even silent movies have words', which is true isn't it? And they have music too, which helps.

Neal: As an illustrator having your own idiosyncratic view of the world is your main weapon, and supposedly what an art director is looking for. On a good day anyway, otherwise they might as well just do it themselves. *LE GUN* is all about daydreams. It's about visual poems. It's a place where we can mess around.

Rob: I like words and I like pictures, but my words come out the wrong way around so I draw pictures.

Would you recommend that students of illustration also develop skills in typography, design and layout?

Bill: You should just call it art. Most illustrators have to learn it all anyway as they go along.

Neal: It's good to work with a designer, but you need to find the right designer. That's what Andrzej Klimowski always used to talk about at college.

What are your thoughts on collaborating with an art director or designer on a project?

Bill: I think maybe people are getting tired of illustration just being used to fill a box on a page. Illustration became very decorative in the 1990s. I think with *LE GUN* we've got a very DIY mentality. No one feels like they can't do anything.

What are your thoughts on the schism between design and illustration?

Alex: Commission an illustrator based on what they can specifically do, not because you need a picture of a dancing pig. Just in the same way as a designer doesn't want to be employed purely on the basis that they can use a Mac. The schism is often created by those who are frustrated because they feel they are not appreciated for what their real skills are.

Chris: At the moment it works in favour of the designer. Designers think they can work as illustrators, but it doesn't work the other way around. What's in it for us?

Matt: Most designers are simply jealous of those with drawing skills. Art directors even more so because their work is so nebulous, so they take out their frustrations by asking for 20,000,001 revisions ('can't you make that one look a bit more "street?"'). Of course that doesn't apply to me. I once did a drawing that looked quite good...

Neal: The illustrator has to bring in something else. A bit of alchemy. Maybe some cider.

Title
Covers from LE GUN
(top right)
Illustrators
Bill Bragg, Alex
Wright, Neal Fox,
Matthew Appleton,
Chris Bianchi and
Rob Greene

Description
A photo from the
LE GUN no.2
launch party (with
hirsute co-founder Rob
Greene in traditional
bowler hat)

The best handmade comic in Cheshire
(a personal perspective on this popular art form)

While growing up in the north of England in the 1960s and 1970s, I was fortunate enough to purchase comics from Northwich market on a weekly basis. The inspirational Jack 'King' Kirby was number one and I became an avid consumer of Silver Age, American and British reprinted Marvel comics. Favourites included *The Mighty Thor*, *The Fantastic Four*, *Captain America*, *X-Men*, *Spiderman*, *Conan the Barbarian*, *The Hulk* and *Sgt. Fury and his Howling Commandos*.

I also read comics and hardback annuals that had accompanying feature film and TV shows such as *Planet of the Apes*, *Star Trek*, *Daktari*, *Tarzan*, *The Outer Limits*, *TV Century 21*, *Dr Who*, *Land of the Giants* and *Voyage to the Bottom of the Sea*. There were always lots of British comics to read and hoard such as *Victor, The Hotspur, Lion, Topper, Beano, Dandy, Commando War Stories in Pictures, Battle Picture Library, Goal* and *Shoot.* Similarly, the comic strips and painterly illustrations in colourful educational magazines such as *Look and Learn, World of Wonder* and *Tell Me Why* were inspiring, as were works of science fiction, the absurd and sheer fantasy.

From about the age of eight I started self-publishing by drawing my own comic strips with felt-tip pens and coloured pencils and, along with my brother, produced dozens of one-off comic books called *ZOOM: The Best Handmade Comic in Cheshire*. *ZOOM* featured the exploits of Sir Cedric and his knights, Sgt. Jackson and his highland regiment, superheroes Wasp Man and Mini Man, the science fiction fantasy of Dat and Kadatons, the World War II action of Call the Commandos, warrior superhero The Super Spartan (who also had his own special issue), the stories of famous battles such as Waterloo, The Somme and The Battle of the Bulge, celebrity profiles such as George Best and Ursula Andress, and a football match strip called Forward the Fraters. The comics were drawn on rolls of wallpaper lining paper, trimmed and bound with Sellotape.

Like many young illustrators, reading, drawing and publishing comics from an early age instilled a passion and obsession for creating my own imaginary worlds and an awareness of storytelling techniques. Although *ZOOM* finally ceased production during the mid 1970s (with punk rock and art school on the horizon), the passion for comic books endures to this day.

Title
Zoom covers and spreads
Illustrator
The author and his brother (aged eight)
Description
The best handmade comic in Cheshire

Installation and interventions

The expanded landscape of illustration also extends to the territory of 3D installations and street-based interventions. Historical precedents are Oskar Schlemmer's *Triadic Ballet*, which was first performed in 1922; Kurt Schwitters' *Merzbau* (1923); Herbert Bayer's exhibition stand kiosks (1924), and Fortunato Depero's pavilion from The International Exhibition of Decorative Arts in Monza (1927), which was known as a work of architectonic typoplasticism.

Through creative collaboration with designers and performing artists, illustrators are generating inventive and imaginative solutions, manipulating a wide range of materials, media and contexts, such as:

3D constructions in metal and wood	**live events**	community arts
murals	conferences	**television and music videos**
mosaics	**museums and exhibition display**	multimedia installations
model making	festivals	**tapestry**
environmental design	**sensory environments**	site-specific signage
special effects	sustainable technology	**corporate events**
costume and theatre design		set design

Peter Nencini

On the facing page is the work of illustrator, designer and educator Peter Nencini, who often works in a collaborative way with production designers to create set designs. Nencini notes that his projects involve:

'collecting, scanning, photographing fragments of objects and architecture, which were then abstracted and redrawn in Illustrator. I like to create a kind of kit, sometimes with an element of modularity, with which to work. Alongside I will make drawings by hand using the same forms and scan them too. I then play a lot and make lots of versions quite intuitively. If the possibilities become too many, too elastic, I will print out the forms and make a hand-cut collage because it feels like a more concrete process. This is then re-scanned and reworked. It's always subject to revision.'

'Communication technology has changed things such a lot. There is no obstacle to anybody publishing their ideas, their writing, their music. Self-authored works output as animation, films or 'zines have become really exciting, culturally influential forms.'
Peter Nencini

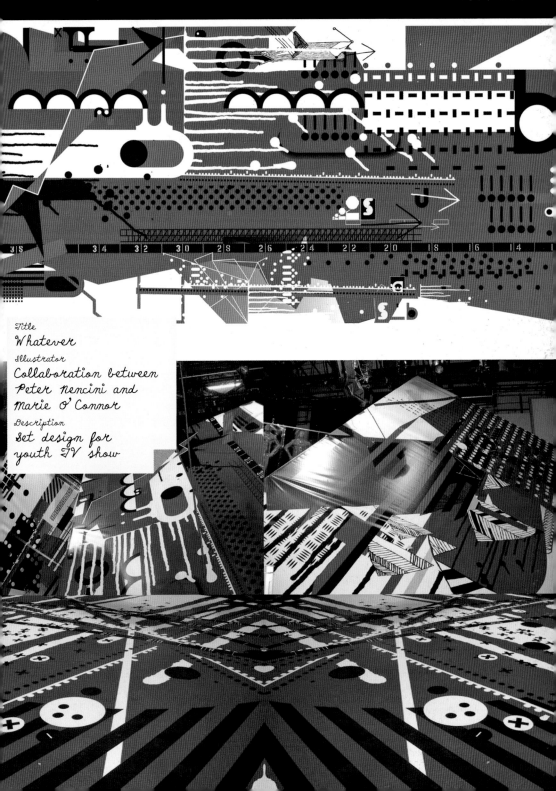

Title
Whatever

Illustrator
Collaboration between Peter nencini and Marie O' Connor

Description
Set design for youth TV show

The Ultimate Holding Company

The Ultimate Holding Company (UHC) is a socially conscious design studio and award-winning art project based in Manchester, UK. Working on a not-for-profit basis, they challenge commercial primacy with politicised art and aim to effect fundamental social change through the creation of new art and design engagement and intervention. UHC have a multidisciplinary, artist-led approach to print, identity, web and event design and have a wide range of clients. Since 2002 they have developed self-initiated projects exploring the built environment, power relations, ecological issues and social injustice.

UHC projects include campaigns to stop the overfishing of eastern European cod stocks (a collaboration with Greenpeace) and to stop the expansion of London's Heathrow airport. The Greenpeace project involved illustrating a parody of Captain Birdseye and the Heathrow piece meticulously hand-traced aeroplane flight paths from radar data into beautiful and disturbingly informative images of pollution.

Other UHC interventions include applying shrouds that feature images of trees with the legend 'trees breathe adverts suck' over every Adshell street-based advert in Manchester. Their Thin Veneer of Democracy (shown opposite), which began as a research project, is an illustrated visual index that maps the knowledge capital and its power relationships on a 16-foot boardroom table. UHC's large-scale works and installations include a collaboration with Platform called Carbon Map (shown on page 104), which displays the global locations and impact of oil and gas production and consumption; Wythenshawe Forever (shown on page 105), which is a community-powered climate change project; and a recycled mapping installation, Tiny Travelling Treasury (pictured below) for Urbis.

Title
Tiny Travelling
Treasury
Illustrator
UHC
Description
Installation, 2007

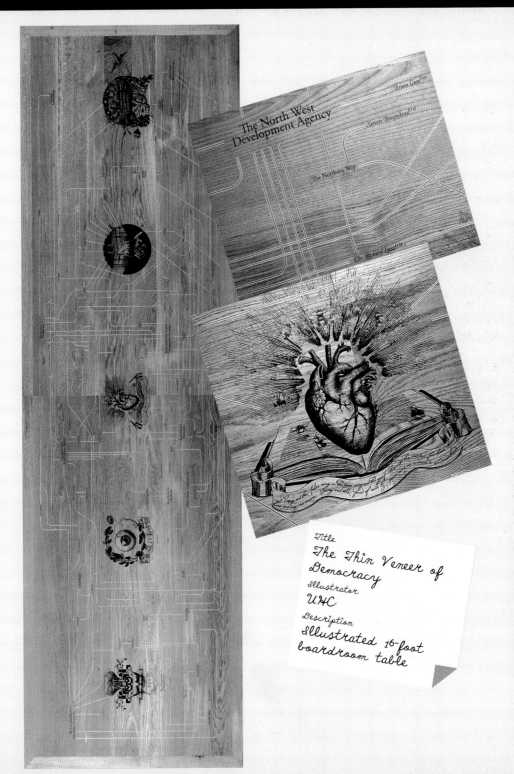

The North West
Development Agency

Bryan Grey (10)

Steven Broomhead (14)

The Northern Way

Cllr Richard Leese (15)

Title
The Thin Veneer of Democracy

Illustrator
UHC

Description
Illustrated 16-foot boardroom table

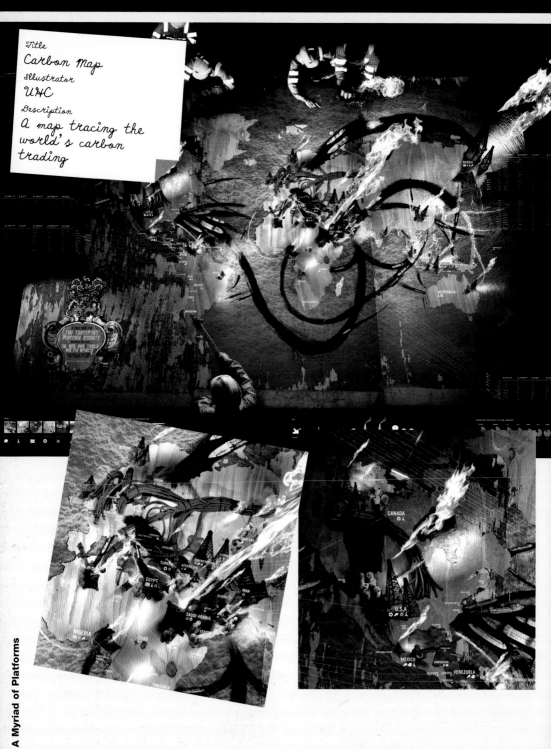

Title
Carbon Map

Illustrator
UHC

Description
A map tracing the world's carbon trading

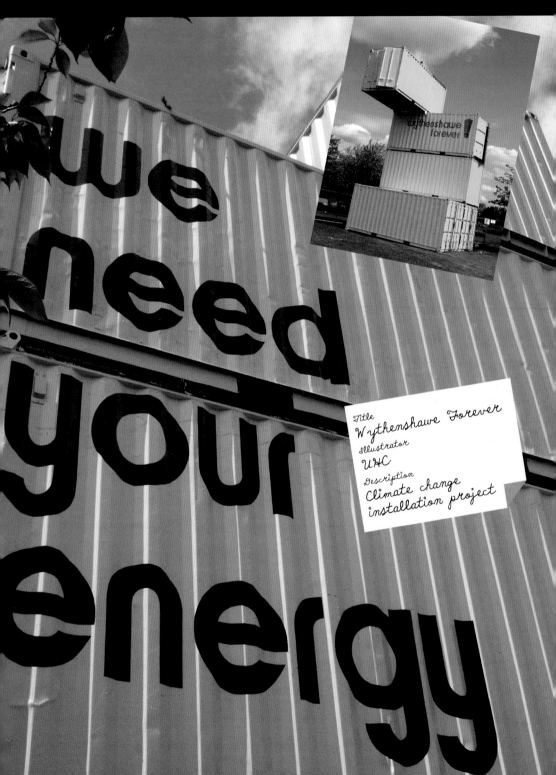

we need your energy

Title
Wythenshawe Forever
Illustrator
UHC
Description
Climate change
installation project

Book jackets

Practically, a jacket is a separate wrapper that protects a book from dust and light, but from the illustrator's perspective, book jackets are essentially small posters that sell the book. Book jackets give visual impact to thrillers, romances, biographies, science fiction, humour and travel titles, as well as a range of other genres.

They represent unique collaborations between publishers, authors and illustrators/designers. Book publishers are increasingly choosing to commission the work of illustrators (rather than photographers) for jacket design, reflecting the growing resurgence of illustration.

Hand-drawn lettering and calligraphy are often combined with symbolic imagery to pictorially evoke and reflect the atmosphere of a book's written contents. Since book jacket illustration first became commonplace in the 1920s (for popular fiction titles) it has been influenced by movements in modern art, from jazz-age imagery and art deco, to expressionism, neo-Victorian style and 1960s pop art to the latest contemporary art.

Many outstanding illustrators have made the book jacket their canvas. Exemplars include: Edward McKnight Kauffer (for Random House and Modern Library), George Salter (for Knopf), Barnett Freedman (for Faber and Faber), Celestino Piatti (for Deutscher Taschenbuch Verlag), Massin (for Gallimard) and John Heartfield (for Malik Verlag).

In the UK, the Folio Society's output has made an important contribution to the illustrated book and visual culture. Charles Ede, whose intention was to publish affordable, well-designed and well-illustrated books, founded the society in 1947. Over 1000 Folio editions have been published, encompassing the works of writers such as Chaucer, Shakespeare and Dickens and all have been interpreted with sensitivity by outstanding illustrators such as Edward Bawden, Charles Keeping, Edward Ardizzone, Lynton Lamb, Nigel Lambourne, Peter Reddick, Val Biro, Derrick Harris, Michael Foreman and Simon Brett.

Title
Portraits of Jazz Legends (far left) and Of Pageants and Picnics (left)
Illustrator
Jonny Hannah
Description
Book jacket designs

'I love doing book covers, I'd never turn one down, it's something I look forward to illustrating.'
Jonny Hannah

Installation and interventions > **Book jackets** > Text in motion

Visual metaphors and graphic wit

Book jackets commonly feature the dynamic use of visual metaphors and graphic wit, as is evident in the text and image combinations of William Addison Dwiggins, Alvin Lustig and Paul Rand.

Penguin paperback books were first launched in 1935 by Sir Allen Lane and have a long association with innovative book cover art. Outstanding examples include artwork directed by Germano Facetti and the illustrator Alan Aldridge. Over the last 70 years, Penguin book covers have been illustrated by some of the world's leading illustrators and typographic designers including Ben Shahn, Michael Foreman, Paul Hogarth, David Gentleman, Romek Marber, Abram Games, Hans Unger, Eric Fraser and Edward Ardizzone. For the company's 70th anniversary celebrations (in 2005), Penguin commissioned 70 covers for a series of miniature books. These covers featured work by leading image-makers such as Marion Deuchars, David Shrigley and Vault 49.

Innovative and contemporary examples of text and image fusion in cover art include the work of Michelle Thompson, whose collages use found letterforms and rubber stamps as elements in her book jackets. Ian Mcmillian and Andy Martin's *Ideas Have Legs* imaginatively combines Ian's prose poems with Andy's found imagery. Also of note are Jenny Griggs's collaged woodblock letterforms for Peter Carey's book covers and Rob Ryan's charming and elaborate paper cut-outs for his own title *This Is For You*.

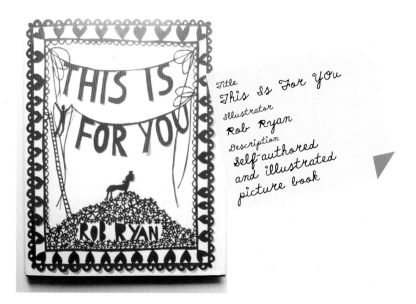

Title
This Is For You
Illustrator
Rob Ryan
Description
Self-authored
and illustrated
picture book

Title
A Taste of the Unexpected
Illustrator
Billie Jean
Description
Book jacket design

'The visual identity of the Dick Bruna books is indelibly etched in my memory. For me, the marriage of Helvetica with Bruna's bold illustrations is the perfect example of the symbiosis between text and imagery. John Tenniel's haunting and definitive illustrations are integral to Lewis Carroll's 'Alice' books, and Phiz's many illustrations for Dickens are inspirational.'
Billie Jean

Installation and interventions > Book jackets > Text in motion

Text in motion

The convergence of technologies, disciplines and channels of communication has enabled the illustrator to engage with many new opportunities. With coherent personal visual languages and a passion for storytelling, illustrators can now express themselves through motion, interactivity, space, time and sound.

In this genre, illustrators can work both independently or as specialists in collaboration with graphic designers, animators, architects, film-makers and software programmers. Alternatively they can operate in a multidisciplinary way taking on new challenges such as: digital and stop-frame animation, film theory and grammar, interactivity, multimedia and sound design. Convergent media, desktop film-making and animation production has been made more affordable and accessible to illustrators by combining software such as After Effects, Flash and Final Cut Pro with their drawing, storytelling and design processes and skills.

This form of animating text and image occurs in a wide range of formats and delivery channels, such as film title sequences, TV graphics and stings, idents, music promos, commercials, site-specific installations, information graphics, internet design, DVD design, animated films, architecture signage, environmental design, viral advertising, mobile hand-held devices and computer games.

Designing for motion requires a feel for narrative, sequence, layout, design, pacing, cinematography and sound and this should be combined with strong ideas and technique. In the field of broadcast identities, MTV has pioneered the way since 1979, commissioning numerous versions of its animated logo. On British television, Channel 4, E4 and BBC Two logos and stings have also been constantly transformed by highly imaginative designs.

Mark Taplin

Illustrator, designer and animator Mark Taplin often brings his distinctive, ironic and sometimes dark sense of humour to his projects. Taplin has created numerous short animated films and stings and all are featured on his website (www.taplabs.com). His projects include work for Virgin Records, MTV, ActionAid, Aids awareness, VH1 and collaborations with fellow members of Black Convoy, Andy Potts (see page 21) and Adrian Johnson (see page 44). Taplin's digital animation work is playful and quirky, fusing 2D and 3D elements and hand-crafted letterforms with fluid and immediate mark-making.

A Myriad of Platforms

Title
Gag cartoons

Illustrator
Al Murphy

Description
Stills from the Paramount Comedy's promotional animation work

Title
Sex, The Dirty Dozen

Illustrator
Mark Taplin

Description
Promotional MTV animation work

Historical inspiration

Historical research into the early days of cinema, in particular the experimental work of the avant-garde during the 1920s and 1930s, can be inspirational. These works include the pioneering films of Marcel Duchamp, Man Ray, Lotte Reiniger, Fernand Léger, Sergei Eisenstein, Dziga Vertov, Oskar Fischinger, Walter Ruttmann, Hans Richter and Viking Eggeling. Non-commercial, independent and experimental film expanded cinema, and early (circa 1950s) computer films and video art is another rich area of study and inspiration.

Designer Saul Bass pioneered the development of the film title sequence as an independent art form during the 1950s and 1960s. Informed by German Expressionism, his title sequences were in themselves short films that related to the visual impact of poster design and served as a metaphor for the whole film. Some of his most influential title sequences were those for *The Man with the Golden Arm*, *Anatomy of a Murder*, *Vertigo*, *Psycho*, *North by Northwest* and, later, *Casino* and *Cape Fear*.

Art designer Robert Brownjohn also integrated text, image and movement imaginatively in the 1960s in the film titles for *From Russia with Love*, *Dr. No*, and *Goldfinger*. Other title sequences of note include Stephen Frankfurt's work for *To Kill a Mockingbird*, Pablo Ferro's illustrative use of typographic design for *The Thomas Crown Affair* and *Dr. Strangelove*, and animator Norman McLaren's *Jack Paar*.

Since the 1990s Kyle Cooper and Imaginary Forces have injected dynamic visual languages into the genre aided by contemporary typographic design and digital innovations with films such as *Se7en*, *The Island of Dr. Moreau*, *Mimic* and *Dawn of the Dead*. Innovative conceptual type play is also evident in Geoff McFetridge's title sequence for *The Virgin Suicides*. Many of the contemporary illustrators featured in the *Basics Illustration* series are embracing motion graphics animation and interactivity; look out for the trailblazing work of Neasden Control Centre (page 27), Black Convoy, David Shrigley, Peepshow Collective, Addictive TV, Tomato, Mark Taplin (page 111), Shynola, *This is* Studio and Pedro Lino.

Opposite Title
The Man with
the Golden Arm
Illustrator
Saul Bass
Description
Promotional poster
(courtesy of the San
Francisco Museum of
Modern Art)

FRANK
SINATRA · ELEANOR
PARKER · KIM
NOVAK

THE
MAN
WITH
THE GOLDEN
ARM

A film by Otto Preminger

an ''untouchable'' theme...
an unusual motion picture!

Project 1: Sound/text installation

Record a series of sounds (for example, the wind, the sea, a bird singing, traffic, an electric generator, the rain, road drills or a helicopter) and interpret them into a narrative installation of letterforms. Choose six completely different sounds and discover poetic associations. Your letterforms should reflect the emotions, moods and feelings conveyed by the sound.

Research and inspiration
Sonic art, installation art, Karlheinz Stockhausen, Abake, Yokoland, Jenny Holzer, Barbara Kruger, Paula Scher, m/m(paris), Tomoko Takahashi, Jeremy Deller, Daniel Eatock, Greyworld, Dan Fern, Sam Winston, Lawrence Weiner, Universal Everything, Crystal Vision, *This is* Studio, Robert Brownjohn, Hyperkit, Graphic Thought Facility, Keiichi Tanaami and Non-Format.

Project 2: Recycled 'zine project

Working in teams of five, collaborate, art direct, illustrate and produce a magazine with a minimum of 20 double-page spreads and a cover. The theme and format is entirely up to you, the only restriction is that you use recycled materials and found objects. Consider allocating roles, target audience flow, pace and consistency of design approach.

Research and inspiration
This is a magazine, *Visionaire*, *Amelia's Magazine*, *Tank*, *The Illustrated Ape*, *Ethical Consumer*, Paul Rand (*Direction*), Neville Brody (*The Face*), Terry Jones (*i-D*), Aubrey Beardsley (*The Yellow Book*), Alexey Brodovitch (*Harper's Bazaar* and *Portfolio*), Herb Lubalin (*Avant Garde*), Rudy VanderLans and Zuzana Licko (*Emigre*), Kurt Schwitters (*MERZ*), John Heartfield (*Die Neue Jugend*), Herbert Spencer (*Typographica*), Kalle Lasn (*Adbusters*), David Carson (*Beach Culture* and *Raygun*), Wyndham Lewis (*BLAST*), Tibor Kalman (*Colors*), Marcel Duchamp (*View*), Josef Müller-Brockmann (*Neue Grafik*), Willy Fleckhaus (*Twen*) and Andy Warhol (*Interview*).

Project 3: A graphic novel

Create a graphic novel that is inspired by the work of William Gibson and/or William Shakespeare. Consider the montage of text and image, the manipulation and relationship of frames, panels, pages, narrative, speech balloons, gesture, perspective, timing, rhythm and lighting.

Research and inspiration
Basics Illustration: Sequential Images by Mark Wigan, *Little Nemo in Slumberland* by Winsor McCay, *Krazy Kat* by George Herriman, *Tintin* by Hergé, *The Spirit* by Will Eisner, *Maus* by Art Spiegelman, *Jimbo* by Gary Panter, *Zap Comix* by Robert Crumb and Jimmy Corrigan *The Smartest Kid on Earth* by Chris Ware.

Project 4: Kinetic word machine

Build a machine that when operated by the user will sequentially display a poem you have written. Use any materials you wish. Consider rotation and interactivity.

Research and inspiration
Dadaism, Surrealism, Outsider Art, Folk Art, Liliane Lijn.

Project 5: The telling line

Read Samuel Taylor Coleridge's *The Rime of the Ancient Mariner* and *Kubla Khan*. Draw a black-and-white, 12-panel comic book inspired by either poem. Generate thumbnails and a dummy book. Be inventive with format, paper stock and navigation. Integrate text and image and remember that a comic has to be read. Use and transform speech balloons to communicate different emotions. Cogitate on the rhythm and timing of the poetry. Consider sense of place, characterisation, analogy, weight and sensitivity of line, sequence, coherent visual language, time, fragmentation, exaggeration, unusual perspectives, lighting, mood, expression and body language.

Research and inspiration
Comics, graphic novels, the Folio Society, *LE GUN*, Paper Rad, Julie Doucet, Mark Beyer, Philip Guston, Mervyn Peake, Lynd Ward, David Jones, Adam Dant, Stéphane Blanquet, Glen Baxter, Ralph Steadman, Fritz Wegner, William Blake, animation and film.

VICIOUS STATEMENTS

IDONTLIKEYOU
INEVERLIKEDYOU
IWASDRUNKAND
YOUWEREEASY

IDONTLOOKATME

IDONTLOVEYOUANYMORE

WHORE

Title
Vicious Statements
Illustrator
Ben Freeman
Description
Four typographical
knives made of
hurtful words

Many of the image-makers featured in this chapter combine physical, handmade and craft-based techniques. Their idiosyncratic and personal approaches are disseminated in a wide range of fluid and open-ended graphic media channels.

Some recycle and reclaim physical objects, transforming and remixing them into collages. Some employ imagination, experimentation, visual metaphors and mnemonics to create letterforms, images and ideas. Some orchestrate emotion and feelings through the manipulation of colour, scale, texture, juxtaposition and contrast, while others deploy parody and pastiche, risk, chance and error. From the painstaking execution of illuminated manuscripts, to the downright painful scratching of text with an X-Acto knife on the naked body by designer Stefan Sagmeister, handmade text is loaded with mystique and connotations of authenticity.

This chapter will:

> **analyse** hand-crafted and digital approaches to type design,
> **introduce** techniques, typographic poetry, cut-ups and concrete poetry,
> **review** historical exemplars and diverse contemporary examples,
> **provide** insights from practitioners and handmade type exercises.

Vicious Statements (left)

Ben Freeman is a contemporary designer who creates letterforms with a wide range of materials. For him, 'the idea dictates the medium of the final piece; I am not in the habit of working in a particular medium for the sake of it. I have made letterforms from wood, wax, brass, powder-coated, laser-etched steel and dead eels. I generally start with ideas in my sketchbook and play around with appropriate media at the production stage. I often use a Mac, but also use craft processes such as casting and metalwork. Materials are extremely important to me, so I have explored many processes, from photography to acid etching.'

Magical letterforms

Letterforms are magical and powerful ways of conveying information, emotion and values. Alphabets illustrate language, integrating the pictorial and typographic. Latin, Greek and Hebrew are phonetic and geometric-based alphabets. Arabic letterforms are cursive and not geometric and Chinese forms are both symbolic and calligraphic.

All over the world, the symbolic and witty interplay of letters and images is a recurring theme. In 19th-century England, keepsakes, almanacs, catalogues and press-out books often featured animated alphabets, rebuses and anthropomorphic figures and letters. Illustrative letterforms can be built from sinuous calligraphy, scratched, embroidered, carved and cut, they can echo the vernacular or outsider art and also reference Victoriana, the graffiti writer or the comic-book artist.

The immediate, spontaneous and emotional qualities of illustrators' hand-drawn letters are evident in a wide range of media and contexts. Handmade and drawn techniques can be mashed up and mixed with the digital to create experimental hybrid forms. Digital tools such as Fontographer, Adobe Streamline, Illustrator, Photoshop, Freehand, Font Studio, Adobe Flash and FontLab have expanded the illustrator's toolkit. Handwriting can be digitised and manipulated, and fonts can easily be designed and embedded. Some illustrators also write their own software and integrate this with older technologies and materials, such as letterpress and silk-screen printing, stencils and photography, neon, foil block and die cutting.

Ed Fella

Ed Fella is a perfect example of someone whose work merges elements of illustration and typographic design to create a highly idiosyncratic personal language. Featured opposite are some of his themed flyers, which Fella uses to promote his lectures and are also given away as souvenirs. Talking about his working practice, Fella comments that he 'never was an illustrator as such, but rather a graphic designer or "layout man" ... I only do my own work now and have done so for some 20 years past. I do spend most of my time designing letterforms ... my techniques and media are still all analogue: pen and ink, but hey, I'm almost 70!'

Book Signing & An Exhibition of Photographs And Posters (Like This One)

GALLERY TALK
SLIDE LECTURE
ED FELLA
LUCY BATES

from against the grain gallery

corner of MAIN and SCHOOL in WELLFLEET Cape COD 00667

STAMP

Title
Magical letterforms
Illustrator
Ed Fella
Description
A selection of posters,
flyers and invitations

'In the recent past I created each piece of work as a complete artwork in watercolour, everything worked out in advance. Although I still work this way, market forces dictate that I now produce more work digitally; drawing, scanning and combining various elements on screen.'
Richard Beards

Title
letterforms
Illustrator
Richard Beards
Description
Creative letterforms

Happy Mothers Day

new logo

same shit company

CHILDREN ARE BORN
WITH THESE ARMS
NOT THESE ARMS

Title
Logos with impact
Illustrator
Mr Bingo
Description
Type and image
working together to
produce visual wit

ABSOLUTELY SHITTING IT

Handcrafted type

From messages daubed on dirt-covered van doors to scrawls on sandy beaches and love hearts cut into trees, visual communication is a physical process. Technical adroitness is achieved through perseverance, play, concentration, practice and the training of hand, eye and brain.

Illustrators, type designers and calligraphers can customise and explore the potential of their tools, including those of traditional lettering, design and carving such as metal pens, quills, reed pens and chisels. Similarly, pen holds, nib positions and angles, writing movements and the viscosity of inks employed can all be explored and experimented with.

Lettering and type design is concerned with the observance and breaking of basic rules. The skeleton structures of alphabets, icon, index and symbol are manipulated in the creation of word-images. The physical construction of letterforms requires freedom of movement and an awareness of:

design principles	gesture	posture	relaxation
contrasts	mark-making	irregularity	focus
rhythm	formal and informal hands	reflection	geometry
structure		intuition	legibility
process	readability	expressive styles	strokes

The handmade mark leaves space for the imagination, for spontaneity and the vital elements of risk and chance, which can lead to a mistake triggering the perfect solution to the brief.

Do it yourself

Examples of integrated fusion of word and image question the idea of 'specialism' and the whole notion of division of labour. Do it yourself is the buzz phrase that sums up much current practice. Contemporary idea- and process-driven strategies involve sampling and mixing digital and traditional techniques.

A generation of designer/illustrators who have used computers since childhood is developing a fascination for analogue techniques as diverse as knitting, tapestry, rug weaving, bookbinding, textiles, embroidery, ceramics, enamelling, metalwork, letterpress and silk-screen printing. Craft, for so long a dirty word in modern design circles, is now considered uber cool. Although the future 'nano' technology promises computers the size and texture of a handkerchief, no doubt illustrators will choose to get out a sewing machine and sew the computers into their collages or clothing!

Title
Jody Barton
Illustration
Illustrator
Jody Barton
Description
Personal promotion
work

Title
Layered text and
image (this page) and
neon text sculpture
(opposite)
Illustrator
Susanna Edwards
Description
Distinctive use
of language

Susanna Edwards

Susanna Edwards works in an interdisciplinary way and tends to work with other people's texts. She collaborates with writers such as Iain Sinclair, interpreting his words into visual forms. When asked about the practice of illustrator as author Edwards comments that 'it's already happening. Lizzie Finn, A Practice for Everyday Life, Peepshow Collective, M/M, *Poetry Fanzine*, Sam Winston, Gilles & Cecilie, myself. Illustrator as designer as artist, it's going on all over the place. I love it when it's done well. Unfortunately too many get seduced by style and aesthetic – it only works when equal attention is spent on content.'

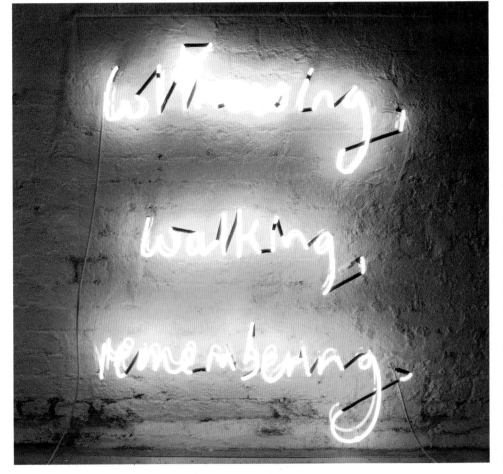

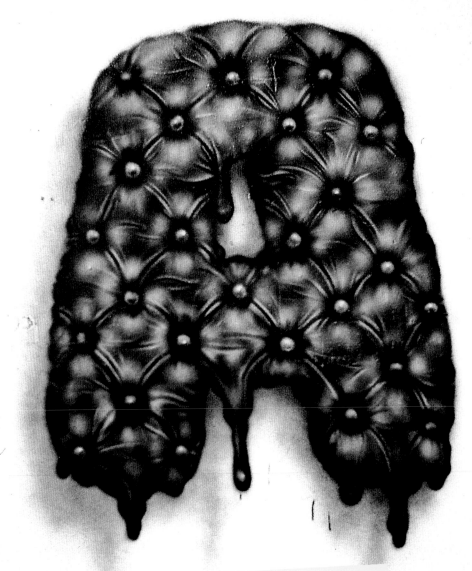

Title
'a'
Illustrator
Nick Walker
Description
An 'a' letterform

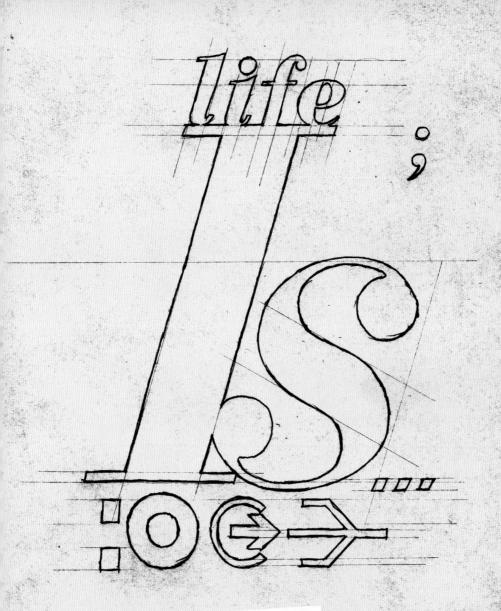

Title
Life is...
Illustrator
Simon Taylor
Description
Hand-drawn
letterforms

OUR
COMPUTER
WHO MONITORS US FROM THE
HEAVENS
HALOED BE THY FUNCTIONS
THY NETWORKS COME
THY WILL BE DONE
ON EARTH AS IT IS IN
CYBERSPACE
GIVE US THIS DAY
OUR DAILY DATA
AND FORGIVE US OUR GLITCHES
AS WE FORGIVE THOSE WHO
HACK AGAINST US
FOR THINE IS THE TECHNOLOGY
THE POWER
AND THE GLORY
UPGRADING THROUGH ETERNITY
COMPUTE

Title
Cyberspace banner
(left)
Illustrator
Rachel McCow-Taylor
Description
Embroidered luddite
era style banner using
golden thread

Title
Please and Thank You
(right)
Illustrator
Alison Casson
Description
Decorative type and
image

The Lord God departed

Title
The Lord God
Departed
Illustrator
Martyn Shouler
Description
Decorative type
sketchbook

Title
Shredded Wheat

Illustrator
John Lundberg

Description
Crop circle work

The contemporary illustrator utilises a broad range of media and techniques, encompassing analogue, handcrafted and digital methods. Tools and materials used can be as varied as found objects, nail polish, oils, household paints, letterpress, stencils, rubber stamps, photograms, typewriters, textiles, fax and badge machines and photographs.

One-man art movement Kurt Schwitters exemplified this visual sampling and collage aesthetic. His working process involved glueing and nailing together paintings that integrated used tram tickets, driftwood, newspapers, buttons and old junk. As the man himself plainly states: 'my name is Kurt Schwitters, I am an artist and I nail my pictures together'.

The handmade images featured here intelligently combine pictures and words, evoking the spirit of William Blake, the Arts and Crafts Movement, Futurism, Dada, Surrealism, Pop Art and Punk.

John Lundberg

John Lundberg has created gigantic examples of text as image using a range of surveying techniques, including a crop circle for Shredded Wheat (pictured opposite), which took a team of four circle makers 14 hours to complete. His work has expanded to include just about any type of large-scale surveying and has been executed using pigment on grass, PVC, sand on beaches, 30 tonnes of rock, and by mowing designs into long grass. The technique he uses to mark out the design are the same across all of the different media; a combination of poles and surveyor's tape mark out the geometry.

In 2005, Lundberg earned himself a second world record by creating the world's largest Sudoku puzzle on the M4 motorway just outside Bristol. His first world record was for creating the largest advert on earth, which was for Thompson Holidays and situated on a runway approach at London's Gatwick airport.

Catalog

Inspired by Kurt Schwitter's *MERZ*, Catalog is a long-term project and graphic concept created by Alex Williamson and Martin O'Neill. During the project they broke down their graphic collections into categories and created typologies to understand the content of their work. Early stages of the project were typographic, focusing on words and typologies. The final pieces they exhibited included posters that visually explored or expressed a category or area of their collection.

Martin O'Neill's collages vary between the textual and the pictorial and are archived in a wide range of vessels such as tobacco tins containing typewriter keys, baskets of pet photos, pint glasses full of numbers and letters, a large box of badly painted Airfix planes, a box full of shopping lists and a cigar box packed with pictures of clouds. The titles of these pieces included *Crayons and Death*, *Inbred Bin*, *Squint Westwood*, *Bikes and Bardot*, *Sad Suits*, *Swivel Chairs and Poofs* and *Dogs and Dice*. Of them, O'Neill says that 'these vessels are a mixture of word association and my own rhyming slang. The titles are drawn over and retitled when the contents change. They work hand in hand with my visual memory and are more of a clue than a definition as to where to find something.'

'The images I'm attracted to usually have an unusual graphic quality coupled with a sense of narrative and will often fit into some kind of graphic fiction that's going on inside my head. I enjoy working with a found image because of its randomness and precisely because I haven't created it. There's a thrill in bastardising and re-contextualising it, making it mine.'

Alex Williamson

Title
mixed-media work
(opposite)
Illustrator
Martin o' neill and
Alex Williamson
Description
Creative collaboration

Sampling and mixing

Title
Mixed-media works

Illustrator
Martin O'Neill and
Alex Williamson

Description
Images taken from the
Catalog exhibition

Typographic poetry

Pattern poetry – poetry in which the lines of text are used to form an image, which usually illustrates the poem's subject or theme – is centuries old. Similarly, the visual play of shapes representing letters is evident in Chinese ideograms, hieroglyphics and picture puzzles. The areas of concrete and pattern poetry can provide the illustrator with a rich source of inspiration for type play.

Non-syntactical visual poetry embraces the absurd and the irrational, the mechanical and the handmade, and the tactile. Here the illustration is not a reflection of the written word, instead the word *is* the illustration. Sometimes the pitch and timbre of musical notation is also employed as a visual metaphor. The reader actively participates with the layers of embedded ideas. 'Spatialism' (or concrete poetry) rips up syntax and semantics through the arrangement of abstracted and disconnected words, letters and sounds.

Historical antecedents include Stéphane Mallarmé's use of blank space in *Un Coup de Dés* (published in 1897) and the visual lyricism of the calligrammatic poems of Guillaume Apollinaire (for example, *Il Pleut*). The English illustrator Edward Lear's work was also a precursor of concrete poetry (consider for example his *A Book of Nonsense* and *Nonsense Songs, Stories, Botany and Alphabets*, which combined limericks and illustration).

The avant-garde works of the Futurists, such as Filippo Tommaso Marinetti, attacked syntax in order to liberate the text, as did the sound poems of Pierre Albert-Birot, Hugo Ball and Tristan Tzara's *Une nuit d'échecs gras*. Lettrism, founded by Isidore Isou in the mid-1940s and Fluxus, founded by George Maciunas, further contributed manifestos, books and art (for example, Maciunas's *Expanded Arts Diagram* in 1966).

'From an early age our taught response is to look at language and unpack the meaning behind it, so even when it is used in an image there is still that pull to read what the text says. This creates a conflict – the image being something you 'look' at whereas the text is something you 'read'. It doesn't sound like much, but the process is done in completely different parts of the brain. And it is around this gap that I base most of my work.'
Sam Winston

Illustrative Text

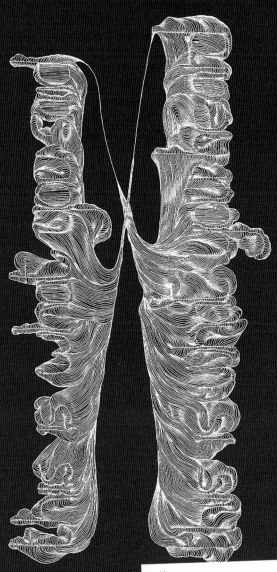

One thinks of around

| Act I – Us | (a play) |

Director: A man walks on stage and finds himself. He defily tries containing it above, whilst he proceeds to stir, it... a man walks in stage and looks at the...

The man says – what can you think here?
The woman says – some thing or you
The woman says – nothing at all
The woman says – nothing
The woman says – something
The man says – nothing

With one look left of the script they fold close and stare at one another. Barry sees and sighs. He comes by and comes on.

The woman says – this is what you wish
The man says – I wish to hide you hand

Title
Hairy Type
Illustrator
Sam Winston
Description
*Blueprint poster
from a leading
typographic poet*

Concrete poetry

Concrete poetry describes those poems in which the typographical arrangement of words is as important in conveying the intended effect as the meaning of the words or their rhythm or rhyme.

Concrete poets include Ian Hamilton Finlay, who has created visual poems in his garden in Lanarkshire, Scotland. Also inspirational is the work of John Furnival who layered words into architectural forms, as can be seen in his six-panel work *Tours de Babel Changés en Ponts* (1965). Poets including Mary Ellen Solt, Ferdinand Kriwet, Dom Sylvester Houédard, Haroldo de Campos and Augusto de Campos are also renowned for their ability to reduce language to its essentials.

The cut up and recomposed text of writers such as William Burroughs and Brion Gysin can also provide the illustrator with inspirational approaches to the fragmentation of text and narrative. Of interest is Brion Gysin's Dial-A-Poem record from 1972 *(I Am That I Am)*. Typographic poetry is also evident in the wit and textured and layered use of type of international street artists and graphic designers such as Alan Fletcher, Katherine McCoy, Stefan Sagmeister, David Carson, Plazm, Simon Taylor (Tomato), Jonathan Barnbrook and in the work of illustrators such as Margaret Cusack and Rian Hughes (featured opposite), whose work is widely recognised for its inventive integration of text and image.

Title
Home Sweet Home
Illustrator
Margaret Cusack
Description
Embroidered
Illustration

Title
Approved, 2006
Illustrator
Kerry Baldry
Description
Video art still

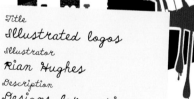

Title
Illustrated logos
Illustrator
Rian Hughes
Description
Designs for various clients

Handmade type projects

Project 1: Guerrilla campaign

Create a handmade, text-based guerrilla advertising campaign to promote a product that is 'you'. Integrate text and image; think crop circles, pavement cleaning stencils, sticker bombing, neon, wool, photocopiers, origami, airships, robots, monumental letterforms, mobile homes, letraset, markers, paper trails, wheat pasting, projections, wigwams, skyscrapers, wooden type, sewing machines, lomo cameras and edible illustration.

Consider visual language and graphic elements such as composition, proportion, scale, hierarchy, syntax, pacing, sound, unity, space, mass, volume, spatial relationships, legibility, craft, contrast, balance, size, consistency, line, texture, variety, juxtaposition.

Research and inspiration
Chris Ware, Ed Fella, Why Not Associates, Ian Wright, Richard Beards, the Clayton Brothers, Richard McGuire, UHC, Banksy, Michael Perry, Wooster Collective, Geoff McFetridge, Deanne Cheuk, Ian 'Swifty' Swift, House Industries, Adam Hayes.

Project 2: Animated brand logo

Create an animated logo for a charity, radio station, sports team, children's TV channel, road safety campaign or political party. The logo is to be deployed in a wide range of applications (for example, interactive media, mobile devices, television, online, printed media and billboards). Consider the importance of simplicity, colour contrast and scale.

Research and inspiration
Cutting edge 3D branding, faux motion, transparent and translucent examples, LogoLounge.com, Fabrica, John Maeda, wolfolins.com, Paula Scher, We Work For Them, Cake.

Project 3: Animated titles

Storyboard and create a title sequence for a TV series that is based on the stories of Hans Christian Andersen.

Research and inspiration
Title sequences, motion graphics, micro films, Psyop, motion theory, Tronic Studio, Norman McLaren, Len Lye, Kyle Cooper, Onedotzero, Shynola, Klaus Haapaniemi, Friends With You, Tim Biskup, Gary Baseman, Hi-ReS.

Project 4: Wit and visual puns

Create 20 illustrations that integrate handcrafted letterforms and images in response to aphorisms such as 'if you see the teeth of the lion, do not think that the lion is smiling to you' (Al Mutanabbi) or 'a lie told often enough becomes the truth' (Vladimir Lenin).

Research and inspiration
Aphorisms, figures of speech, proverbs, epigrams, paradox, simile, analogy, conceptual illustration.

Project 5: Enchanting images

Choose one of the following classic stories to illustrate: *Alice in Wonderland, Snow White, The Emperor's New Clothes, Cinderella, Little Red Riding Hood, Peter Pan* or *The Wind in the Willows*.

Design the front cover and ten double-page spreads that each represent key aspects of the story. Make appropriate use of typography and reference observational and imaginative drawing, characterisation and composition. The book's format, paper stock and materials are your decision.

Research and inspiration
Walter Crane, Kate Greenaway, Sir John Tenniel, Beatrix Potter, Randolph Caldecott, Maurice Sendak, Edward Arizzone, Ernest Shepard, AB Frost, Howard Pyle, Arthur Rackham, Miroslav Sasek, Quentin Blake, Raymond Briggs, Sara Fanelli, Tony Ross, Michael Foreman, Lauren Child, Paula Rego, Mabel Lucie Attwell, Mervyn Peake.

Project 6: Below the line

Using handmade letterforms rebrand a product or service of your choice. Utilise strategies such as direct mail, printed campaign materials, ambient media formats, mobile marketing interventions and stealth and viral advertising.

Research and inspiration
Neckface, KAWS, Shepard Fairey, Twist, ESPO, Dondi White, Amaze, Revs, WK INTERACT, Seen, Earsnot (Irak), Space Invader, Swoon, Germs.

Title
Cakes & Ale Press
Illustrator
Jonny Hannah
Description
Promotional exhibition
poster

A paradigm shift is occurring in illustration as the traditional boundaries of creative art forms are disappearing. Illustration is flourishing, with inspiration drawn from skate culture, graffiti, cinema, politics, street art, environmental issues, semiotics, architecture, mathematics, folk art, graphic design, history, contemporary art, music graphics and much more besides.

Evocative, personal and ideas-led strategies are challenging the formulaic approaches and vacuity of much illustration, design and fine art. A priority for illustrators is playfulness and the enjoyment of creating handcrafted images using both analogue and digital techniques.

Fundamental, observational skills and drawing in its broadest sense underpin much illustration education. This back-to-basics approach is enhanced by mixing and blending digital methods and tools such as digital cameras, scanners, After Effects, Flash, Photoshop, Final Cut Pro, InDesign and Illustrator, Painter, 3D studio Max and Maya.

The illustration spectrum is not medium-specific; everything can be a tool utilised to express ideas, for example, sketchbooks, sound recording equipment, gocco printers, badge machines, graphics tablets, pencils, linocuts, photographs, rubber stamps, flip books, physical spaces, murals, installations, sensory environments, body painting and much, much more.

The paradigm shift in illustration is now producing maverick and pragmatic collectives that are establishing their own small and successful multidisciplinary studios, generating personal self-initiated projects and gaining exposure and commissions from editorial, publishing and corporate clients.

This chapter will:

> **introduce** the outlet of music and nightclub industry illustration,
> **explore** historical precedents and contemporary strategies,
> **present** contemporary examples of flyer art and music packaging,
> **provide** informative commentary from leading illustrator Paul Burgess.

Cakes & Ale Press (left)

This imprint is Jonny Hannah's very own cottage industry through which he produces highly collectable and editioned screen-printed books, posters, prints and boxed sets. Hannah's work also appears in the *Daily Telegraph*, the *New York Times* and the *St. Kilda Courier*.

Sound and vision

Music graphics are designed not only to attract potential purchasers by synthesising text, image and concepts, but also to communicate the values associated with the musician and the musical genre. Much like posters, record sleeves have become iconic artefacts reflecting the cultural concerns and attitudes of their time.

Record-sleeve artwork has inspired and influenced the development of graphic art and introduced generations to the world of illustration. Artists as diverse as Peter Blake, Joseph Beuys, Keith Haring, Barbara Kruger, Sol LeWitt, Andy Warhol and Gerhard Richter have all created images for record sleeves.

During the 1980s, the eye-catching and poster-like sleeves were largely replaced by the smaller format CD. The direct visual impact of the smaller format was enhanced by the sequential and narrative opportunities provided by the CD jewel case. The CD format itself is now being superseded by electronic downloads, but even so, vinyl records, with their tactile and visual sleeves, have become highly desirable collectors' items for the digital generation.

The design of music packaging has not died, but instead continues to evolve and adapt to a wide range of delivery media. Illustrated visual content is commonly provided to brand and promote music artists through websites, microsites, printed and online magazines, stage and set design, limited-edition packaging, merchandise such as badges and T-shirts, banner ads, music videos and internet and mobile phone downloads.

Title
CD and record sleeves
Illustrator
Mark Wigan
Description
Tommy Musto for
Deconstruction (far
left), A Guy Called
Gerald for CBS Sony
(left), and Frankie
Bones and Animated
and Pacific State for
Deviant Records (this
page)

DINGWALLS
CAMDEN LOCK LONDON NW1

MONDAY 19th OCTOBER 1998
QUICKSPACE
AND SPECIAL GUESTS
SOLEX
PLUS DJS

DOORS 7:30

KITTY KITTY XMAS EXTRAVAGANZA 17th

QUICK
LIGAM
NOYA

THE SAUSAGE MACHINE
PLAYS DISGUSTING MUSIC
WHITE HORSE, HAMPSTEAD

moonshake

EARWIG

SAT 20 JULY

Title
Various
Illustrator
Dan @ The Mangle
Description
Gig poster and record
label designs

Often a band or record label's visual identity will be synonymous with the work of an image-maker. Such is the case with Jim Flora's work for RCA; David Stone Martin for Blue Note Records; Hipgnosis for Pink Floyd, Led Zeppelin and Yes; Cal Schenkel's stage sets, lighting, adverts and sleeves for Frank Zappa; Pedro Bell for Funkadelic; Vaughan Oliver for 4AD; Peter Saville, 8vo and Central Station for Factory Records, and Jamie Hewlett's animation and designs for Gorillaz.

Designers and illustrators continue to create highly imaginative and inventive work in this area, especially for limited-edition records and small labels. Some are also branching out and making their own music, stage sets, costumes and handmade merchandise. Exemplars include Grandpeople's designs for Melektronikk, illustrator/designer/film-maker/musician Kim Hiorthøy for Rune Grammofon, the multidisciplinary Chicks on Speed, Yokoland for Metronomicon Audio label and Non-Format for Lo Recordings.

Title
CD Sleeves
Illustrator
Richard May
Description
Artwork for indie bands Cuban Crime and Punish the Atom

Title
Basement Beat Jazz
Illustrator
Chris Watson
Description
Limited-edition poster

Title
Guest artist for the
British Fashion
Council
Illustrator
Andrew Foster
Description
Illustrations for
fashion week

'Often I'll be thinking "what the hell am I going to do with this?".
Convinced that this time I've got absolutely nothing, I'll read
it a second time, underlining any word that might trigger a good
idea and making small sketches in the margins. Before long I'll have
a handful of quick sketches to pick from. Sometimes one idea will
click straight away, often the first idea is the best, you have to learn
to trust your instinct.'
Chris Watson

Paul Burgess

Collage artist, illustrator and designer Paul Burgess has a career that spans over 20 years. His projects have included book jackets for Vintage Books, poster artworks for Julien Temple's Sex Pistols film *The Filth and the Fury,* a variety of music industry work and a list of clients that includes TopShop, *Design Week*, *GQ* magazine and John Lydon.

What are your thoughts on the interpretation of text in illustration?

Paul: Any form of text used within illustration should sit well with the image. It should be seen as an equal element alongside composition, colour and content. Text should not fight with the image, but embrace it, tickle it and cuddle it.

Do you design letterforms as an element within your illustrations?

Paul: No, I like a much rougher approach. I like to hand-paint text with a paint brush, or use rubber stamps, found lettering or collage.

Would you recommend that students of illustration also develop skills in typography, design and layout?

Paul: Yes, this is very important. Try not to be frightened of type, or page layout. Start by treating letterforms as simple shapes and moving them around the page. Be playful, and always say to yourself, there is no right or wrong way of doing this. If you are using the computer, start by only using three or four typefaces, otherwise it gets far too confusing.

What techniques and media do you use to create letterforms in your illustrations?

Paul: I use found type, hand-painted type, stencils and rubber stamps, I then scan these into the Mac and play around with them. Sometimes I will use set type, but not very often. The text I use usually comes from conversations, song lyrics or things I have found in the street. For me I find this more exciting. I use the computer just like a photocopier, usually it is just a tool to enlarge, reduce or change the colour of the type.

Title
We got Soul
Illustrator
Paul Burgess
Description
Personal work

itle
ollages (left and far
ft)
lustrator
aul Burgess

Title
The Filth and the
Fury
Illustrator
Paul Burgess
Description
Poster and cover art
for Julien Temple's
(2001) documentary
film

UNSEEN AND UNCUT

THE FILTH AND THE FURY
A SEX PISTOLS FILM
DIRECTED BY JULIEN TEMPLE

SEX PISTOLS
PISTOLS

Club flyers

Another important artefact in the context of design for music is the club flyer. For students of illustration and graphic design, flyers can provide creative freedom, the experience of working with printers and exposure for their work.

In the early 1980s, on graduation from a graphic design BA course, flyers for underground nightclubs, such as the Warehouse at the Electric Ballroom in Camden Town, became some of the author's first commissions. At that time one would design, illustrate, photocopy and distribute the flyers in pubs, shops and clubs. Once the artwork on the flyers gained recognition amongst its audience, commissions for more varied work followed.

The communication of events via flyers and leaflets has a long history and includes radical pamphlets, wartime propaganda, promotional material for avant-garde art movements and gig promotion material. The design and integration of text and image in these often reflected the aesthetic of the time and the visual languages of the sub- and counter-cultural events that they publicised; from the do it yourself, cut 'n' paste, photocopied punk aesthetic of the late 1970s, to the fluorescent 1980s and 1990s rave graphics, and from the corporate identities of the superclubs such as The Hacienda, Cream and the Ministry of Sound, to today's contemporary flyers emailed to social networking sites and mobile phones.

Illustrators and designers who have produced highly original work in this genre include Andrew Rae, Peter Saville, Simon Taylor, Stephen Fowler, Jason Brooks, Dave Little, James Jarvis, Graham Rounthwaite, Paul Khera, Elliot Thoburn, James Joyce, Kate Moross and Martin Fewell.

Title
Club flyers
Illustrator
Mark Wigan
Description
assorted flyers from
the archive

'I think it's important (as a creative individual) to work on personal projects away from the constraints of a given commercial brief. It's often the hardest thing to do, but ultimately the most satisfying...

Title
It's Bigger Than
Illustrator
James Joyce (Joycey)
Description
Assorted club flyers

...I'm both a graphic designer and an illustrator and so often they overlap and work harmoniously together. Sometimes the two need to be separate though; certain briefs require a pure graphic design approach and others an illustrative approach, whichever answers the question most effectively.'
James Joyce (aka Joycey)

Project 1: Pick and mix for the thinking eye

Have fun and immerse yourself in some or all of these projects. Draw, play, create worlds, think conceptually, use your imagination and make great art for people.

Create a series of postage stamps on the theme of endangered species.

Design a typographic self-portrait utilising text as image.

Create an image entirely from found and collaged letterforms that is based on the theme of overheard conversations.

Design a poster for a theatre production of Shakespeare's Romeo and Juliet. Ensure that you include appropriate typographic information.

Create a logotype, re-brand and ambient advertising campaign for the World Wildlife Fund.

Design a cross-media advertising campaign to promote recycling and sustainability.

Produce a storyboard and animated title sequence for a classic 1940s or 1950s film noir or a science fiction film.

Create a series of portraits for a magazine article or a pack of cards (such as most wanted criminals, sports stars, famous artists, film stars, politicians or pop stars).

Draw a series of four reportage illustrations for a newspaper or e-zine: choose your own theme and write and draw your own story.

Create character designs, avatars, costumes, accessories, landscapes and architecture for an online virtual world.

Design a front cover and six spot illustrations for a Greenpeace or Amnesty International company report.

Illustrate the metaphor 'roadmap to peace'.

Design a poster, programme, set design and costumes for an opera, stage musical, fringe theatre, play, or ballet

Construct a zoetrope, a pop-up book or puppet show that incorporates a fable, myth or legend.

Create a book of illustrations based on one of the following themes: dinosaurs, famous battles, insects or pirates.

Produce a 'weird weather' series of illustrations depicting floods, storms, tidal waves and tornados.

Design a travel poster for a travel agency called 'Carbon Footprint'.

Produce a typographic manifesto that represents your ethical and political views.

Create a cover for a ghost storybook.

Design an advent calendar.

Create an alphabet book for children.

Design a poster for Bizet's *Carmen*.

Research and inspiration

The AOI, The Society of Illustrators, *American Illustration*, *Varoom*, *Communication Arts*, *Computer Arts*, *Illustration Magazine*, *3x3* magazine, D&AD, The Central Illustration Agency, Advocate Art, Folio, Synergy, Jelly and Big Active.

Graphic Art Zeitgeist

Title
Walk don't walk
Photographer
Damilola Odusote
Description
street art in NYC

Conclusion

From the visceral to the whimsical and the absurd to the oblique, illustration is proving an interesting portal from which to investigate new strategies for the arts. The orchestrating of images and words to tell stories, educate, agitate, inform, amuse, persuade and entertain is taking place in the cracks between subject disciplines and the art and design worlds. It is within this area that new visual languages and practices have challenged traditional perceptions and hierarchies.

The illustrator's purpose is to illuminate, clarify and elucidate the text. Whether she/he does this as a servant of the text, an artist, designer, shaman, semiotician, curator, comedian, entrepreneur, author, appropriator, editor, philosopher, director, animator, choreographer, politician or typographer (combine, delete and add as you wish) is entirely up to the individual.

This book has explored the relationship between text and image from the illustrator's point of view and it has provided stunning images, unique insights, techniques, processes and methodologies from exemplars of contemporary practice. Insights that will hopefully inspire you and challenge your definitions of the subject. The issues investigated here will aid you in positioning your own work within the current cultural, social and political context of visual communication.

Illustration is an important applied art form and a powerful tool of visual communication. Illustrators must combine their imaginative personal vision, techniques and ideas with strong underlying design skills.

Title
Oblique storytelling
Illustrator
Simone Lia
Description
Scenes from an
imaginary world

Glossary

This subjective glossary, a synthesis of old and new with no distinction between theory, practice and techniques, is an attempt to encourage a dialogue between two disciplines – illustration and graphic design – interlinked by the realities of industry, cooperation and digital technology.

1860s
A period described as the 'golden age of British professional illustration'. The 1860s saw developments in print technology, distribution and the publication of affordable books and periodicals. Illustrators working in this period included Cruikshank, Doyle, Tenniel, Keene, Pinwell, Hughes, Millais, Boyd Houghton and the Pre-Raphaelite illustrators such as Dante Gabriel Rossetti.

Adbusters
An influential magazine founded by Kalle Lasn, which takes a critical stance on advertising and consumerism, promoting culture jamming, 'uncommercials' and 'subvertising'.

Cursive
Letterforms that flow as they might in handwriting (such as italics).

Digital type formats
Incorporating PostScript (developed by Adobe Systems Inc. in 1983), TrueType (developed by Apple and Microsoft in the late 1980s), and OpenType (developed by Microsoft and Adobe in 1997 for cross-platform use).

Emigre
An influential journal and digital type foundry launched by Rudy VanderLans (1984) and later featuring work by Zuzana Licko. Emigre's experimental fonts were informed by the introduction of the Apple Macintosh in 1984.

Expressionist (book illustration)
Powerful illustration reflecting the horrors of the First World War, the upheaval of the 1917 Russian Revolution and the rejection of bourgeois society. Evident in the work of Käthe Kollwitz, Otto Dix, Max Beckmann, George Grosz and the Die Brücke (1905–1913), and artists such as Oskar Kokoschka and Ernst Ludwig Kirchner.

Font
The physical weight, size or style of a typeface or character. Any material can be used to create a font including hand-rendered type or code and font generation programs such as Fontographer and FontLab.

Graphic design
A term first used by William Addison Dwiggins in 1922 in the context of design for print. After the Second World War the term started to be used widely in professional and educational fields. Graphic design is an interdisciplinary and hybrid activity that involves organising words and images, and acts as an intermediary with clients and specialists. Graphic design informs, persuades, entertains, instructs, provokes and problem-solves.

Head, heart and hand
Professor Richard Guyatt's analysis of a design and its three interrelated elements. Taken from *Anatomy of Design* (1951): 'the head provides logic, the heart emotional stimulus, the hand with skill gives form to the design'.

Illustrator/designer
There are many that fit this description. Historical precedents include Eric Ravilious (1903–1942) and Edward Bawden (1903–1989) from the UK. Also of note is New York's Push Pin studio with their publications, editorial, advertising design and illustration. The Polish poster designers of the 1960s and the Japanese graphic artists of the 1970s also fit this description.

Industry
'Life without industry is sin and industry without art brutality' – a quote from John Ruskin reflecting the philosophy of the Arts and Crafts movement.

Legibility
The ease with which the reader can decipher and distinguish typeforms and information.

Post-structuralism
Derived from 1960s French critical theory, post-structuralism is a critical response to structuralism. Writers such as Jacques Derrida, Michel Foucault, Julia Kristeva and Roland Barthes questioned how knowledge is made and argued that the interpretation of text depends on the identity of the reader.

Readability
The reader's ability to understand the message or emotions conveyed by illustrator or designer. The composition of text and image on page or screen or in an environment needs to be coherent in its use of visual hierarchy and language.

Sans serif
A typeface without serifs (terminal strokes). Examples include Gill Sans by Eric Gill (1928), Futura by Paul Renner (1927–29), and Helvetica by Max Miedinger and Edouard Hoffmann (1957).

Text
Printed or written matter (such as the body copy that forms the main text of a publication). Text can also be the words of an author.

Typefaces
A typeface usually comprises an alphabet of letters, numerals, and punctuation marks. Typefaces are generally characterised as being of one of four groups:
Block: based on Middle Ages writing. Also called Black Letter, Old English, Broken or Gothic typefaces. Roman: decorative serif typefaces and old style variations (such as Bembo, Baskerville, Bodoni, Clarendon and Egyptian (Slab Serif)). Gothic: broken script, Fraktur, Textura, sans serif and display text (such as Grotesque and Helvetica).
Script: decorative typefaces derived from handwriting

Typography
Conveying messages through the design, selection and composition of typefaces. Like illustration, typography is constantly evolving and concerns the manipulation of visual languages in many contexts including typefaces, logotypes, information design and sign systems, trademarks or concrete poetry.

Title
Lecture poster (top) and magazine cover design (bottom)
Illustrator
Billie Jean

What are your thoughts on the interpretation of text in illustration?

'My initial influences, the things that really opened my eyes to art, were record covers, psychedelic posters and pop art, all integrated type with image. Right from the start I made images with text. By the time I got to college I thought this must make me a graphic designer, but then I realised that what I loved doing was art directing my own work. When I started illustrating I was amazed at the terrible type that was plonked on top of my artwork, so increasingly I did my own type. For me, type is of equal importance to any other element of a picture, it should be intrinsic to the design, not an afterthought or appendage.'
Michael Gillette

'I like to think of illustrators not only visually interpreting given text, as has been our traditional role, but being actively involved in its origination. I hope that more and more illustrators will investigate language and typography, allowing us to feel confident enough to write text and design typographically, not just as a bolt-on to our images, but as part of a more expansive graphic design and journalistic role. If we can view the role of text/typography as something that is an essential part of illustration we don't need to be purely a stylistic service provider. Many illustrators seem to view text as decoration or something that illustration follows. I would like to see illustrators who understand language, punctuation, typography and visual grammar become more the norm. I would hope that these new illustrators are happy to still call themselves illustrators.'
Paul Bowman

'I'm a big fan of text in illustration, the more integrated with the image the better (even to the point of illegibility) as long as the result is striking.'
Andy Potts

What are your thoughts on the schism between design and illustration?

'I have always felt that since computers have become a major tool to illustrators, the gap between the two fields has narrowed to produce some of the most beautiful and exciting work. Most of the books I buy are graphic design books.'
Brett Ryder

'Design incorporates many things, one of which is illustration. It also uses photography, typography, video, sound, etc. So, I'm not sure how strong the schism really is from a modern design perspective. I would, however, love to see more illustrators tackling design and typography in their own work and crossing the schism from that side.'
Kristian Olson

'More and more people are developing skills in both disciplines. There is much more understanding of each other's fields; designers are illustrating and illustrators are designing.'
Nishant Choksi

'There isn't one … in our eyes anyway! Maybe it's just because we feel comfy in the treacherous waters in between.'
John McFaul

Text and Image

What are your thoughts on telling stories in pictures, narrative illustration and text and image working in harmony?

'Successful integration of text within an illustration can create a far greater emotional response for the viewer. Unlike moving image and sound, a static illustration has to achieve its response with far less ammo at its fingertips. People like Paul Davis and David Shrigley achieve this perfectly, with neither text nor image taking precedence over the other, but both creating an immediate, and lasting visual impact.'
Paul Willoughby

What are your thoughts on the illustrator as author, taking control of the whole process?

'I'm very keen on this, I think it means you can push boundaries a bit as you don't have so many commercial constraints and there's not the feeling that you have to please somebody else. I've done quite a few self-published book projects and they often develop into real jobs when seen by clients who then want something similar. However, when it comes to real work they are always watered down due to all the outside influences – the designer/art directors are usually happy, but the end client often has his or her own agenda, understandably so! I think it's important to do some work for yourself.'
Andy Smith

'Control! Being in total control? How profitable and creative is it being in total control? Does the project get better and does the illustration become more interesting because you take total control of the whole process? I don't think so. For me, being the author means being too close to the project and this can often result in a 'woods for the trees' situation arising. Essentially, I think it brings with it too many factors to consider and by implication of having total control you have too much creative choice.'
Russell Walker

'I guess I don't think of myself as an illustrator or author per se. I think of myself as an artist who uses words and pictures to communicate so it's natural for me to work in this way. But in speaking of taking control of the whole process, if I'm working with a publisher I do take an interest in the design and paper used, but at the end of the day when working as part of a group, it's a lot about saying what you think and then letting go of your ideas. The only other alternative is to do it yourself.'
Simone Lia

'I enjoy it when a client has the confidence in you to take control of the whole project; illustration, type and layout. It makes for a more consistent and coherent piece of work. On the other hand, it's very satisfying to see your illustration handled well by a designer, laid out with great type in ways you wouldn't have considered.'
Andy Potts

Do you design letterforms as an element within your illustrations?

'Sometimes I will experiment with a few elements to come up with something new, but mainly the text that I use will have come directly from somewhere I have been drawing – maybe from a menu on a wall or from someone's T-shirt or from a leaflet lying on the floor. I do quite a lot of location drawing and I'm always recording things, which I suppose has helped me to assemble a personal theory of what is appropriate and what is not appropriate to use within my work. I feel that it all has to somehow fit together and be relevant.'
Cath Elliot

'It depends on what the piece requires. My "jazz" book needed a complete typeface, so I cut one for it. But sometimes you instinctively know what type form will look good where. It can be based on an existing typeface, Rockwell Shadow perhaps. Or I might nick something from Ravilious or Barnett Freedman. Or it could be three dawbs of paint to make an "A". It just depends. If, for example, I'm drawing a piece about cowboys, a letterform such as Playbill is ideal. Or a letter with a wobbly edge can suggest something scary and ghostly. Certain shapes of letters go with certain themes. But that's not to say you can't go in the opposite direction as well. It's as Elizabeth David once said about cooking, you must first learn the rules, in order to break them.'
Jonny Hannah

What are your thoughts on collaborating with an art director or designer on a project?

'I often hear illustrators talk about designers/art directors as the enemy. Yes there are some terrible art directors and designers who have no idea about commissioning, the integrity of an illustrator's work or what the relationship should be about. This obviously screws up any creative process. However, let's not forget that there are some truly dreadful illustrators who have no identity, personality or vision of practice. They don't understand the true potential and power of being an illustrator. A good relationship helps to develop and improve both people's work and ultimately the article/product you are selling.'
Andrew Foster

'This really just depends on the flexibility of the creative you are working with. The more open they are to your ideas, the easier the project becomes. It can definitely improve your work if carried out with the right people, it's always good to have a few opinions coming in on the work. Sometimes they can be baddies though!'
John McFaul

'This is all about relationship, communication and being part of a team. With any group work, the experience will always be different depending on the people in your team and your own attitude.'
Simone Lia

Text and Image

Would you recommend that students of illustration also develop skills in typography, design and layout?

'Absolutely. And I think design students should develop the means to create imagery. To me illustration and graphic design is the same thing. I fail to see what good a forced, constructed, separation could bring. Layout and design are both already something all illustrators work with by default. An illustration is a layout, a design, in itself. Is it not? Looking at it from the other way round, type is more than just text; illustration is built in. A text set in two different typefaces tells two very different stories. Once thoughts like these set the parameters for illustration and graphic design, separation becomes hard to understand and far from the actual everyday work. Browsing through the works of legends like Paul Rand, Saul Bass, Zero and so on underlines this. Were they all illustrators? Or graphic designers?'
Jonas Bergstrand

'Yes, most definitely. It's really important to have some understanding of typography and the design process. I always feel like an old fart when espousing this theory to illustration students. It's not really an urgent concern for them. They're far more interested in digital animation, web design and making cute figurines and I don't blame them!'
Billie Jean

'I'm glad that old boundaries are eroding between disciplines like design and illustration. Artists have always disregarded rules and stolen things from unexpected places; Picasso took tribal masks and Miro stole from *Krazy Kat* comic. I think design and illustration are stealing from each other more than ever. First cheap colour printing, then the web have made a wealth of visual material readily available. All of pop culture history is easily available one way or another; for example, you'd be hard pushed to find a book on Saul Bass, but there are thousands of his images online and his style has filtered down the pop pyramid from last year's retro-cool gig posters to today where TV bubblegum commercials are now emulating his letter style. Illustration students should have access to learning typography, animation, layout, composition and colour theory, as well as letterpress, printmaking and photography.'
Chris Watson

'We need to examine other forms of communication if we are to grow. Interestingly, I have found that any illustrator who learns typography or crosses disciplines inevitably wants to be called something other than an illustrator. New abilities for illustrators become a kind of class mobility. A shame.'
Paul Bowman

'These skills should be a prerequisite for illustrators; the more you understand the mechanics of a page and its layout, the greater integrity your response will have.'
Paul Willoughby

Books

Baines, P.
Penguin by Design: A Cover Story 1935–2005
Penguin Books (2005)

Baines, P. and Haslam, A.
Type & Typography
Laurence King (2005)

Barthes, R.
Image, Music, Text
Hill and Wang (1977)

Bell, R. and Sinclair, M.
Pictures and Words: New Comic Art and Narrative Illustration
Laurence King (2005)

Dalby, R.
The Golden Age of Children's Book Illustration
Book Sales (2001)

Ellison, A.
The Complete Guide to Digital Type
Laurence King (2006)

Eskilson, S.J.
Graphic Design: A New History
Laurence King (2007)

Foster, J.
New Masters of Poster Design: Poster Design for the Next Century
Rockport Publishers Inc. (2006)

Gravett, P.
Graphic Novels: Everything You Need to Know
Collins Design (2005)

Hanson, T.S.
The Design Legacy of George Salter
Princeton Architectural Press (2005)

Heller, S. and Chwast, S.
Graphic Style: From Victorian to Post-Modern
Abrams (1988)

Heller, S. and Ilic, N.
Handwritten: Expressive Lettering in the Digital Age
Thames & Hudson (2004)

Hodnett, E.
Image and Text: Studies of the Illustration of English Literature
Scolar Press (1982)

Kostelanetz, R. (Ed.)
Imaged Words & Worded Images
Outerbridge & Dienstfrey (1970)

Kostelanetz, R. (Ed.)
Text-Sound Texts
Morrow & Co. (1980)

Male, A.
Illustration: A Theoretical and Contextual Perspective
AVA Publishing SA (2007)

Massin
Letter & Image
Studio Vista (1970)

McCullough, K.
Concrete Poetry: An Annotated International Bibliography
Troy NY: Whitston (1989)

Text and Image

Annuals

Pennell, J.
A New Illustrator: Aubrey Beardsley
The Studio Issue No. 1 (1893)

Poyner, R. and Spencer, H.
Pioneers of Modern Typography
Lund Humphries (2004)

Sabin, R.
Comics, Comix and Graphic Novels
Phaidon Press (2001)

Shahn, B.
Love and Joy About Letters
Grossman Publishing (1963)

Shulevitz, U.
Writing with Pictures
Watson-Guptill (1985)

Sullivan, E.J.
The Art of Illustration
Chapman and Hall Ltd. (1921)

Tomato
Process: A Tomato Project
Thames & Hudson (1996)

Varnum, R. and Gibbons, C.
The Language of Comics, Word and Image
University Press of Mississippi (2002)

Wainwright, A.W.
Pictorial Guides to the Lakeland Fells
Frances Lincoln (2003)

Zeegen, L. and Crush
The Fundamentals of Illustration
AVA Publishing SA (2005)

The Penrose Graphic Arts
International Annuals
(from the 1960s and 1970s)

The European Illustration
Yearbooks
(1970s and 1980s)

Graphis Annuals
(1950s onwards)

The Illustrator's Annual
(The Society of Illustrators)

American Illustration
(HarperCollins International)

The Association of Illustrator's
Images Annual
(Association of Illustrators)

Writers' and Artists' Yearbook
(A&C Black)

Children's Writers' and
Artists' Yearbook
(A&C Black)

Periodicals

Amelia's Magazine, Line, Illustration, AOI Journal / Varoom, Communication Arts, The Illustrated Ape, LE GUN, Juxtapoz, EYE, Adbusters, Design Week, Graphis, Creative Review, Bionic Arm, Peel, Refill, Found, Little White Lies, Lodown, Arty, World War 3 Illustrated, Rugged, Craphound, Brut, Lunch, ModArt magazine, Super7, Play, Pop, Graff It!, Graphotism, Belio, Atmosphere, Crash, Bust, Beat Specialten, The Believer, Form, Relax, Stranger, Draft, Wonderland, Res, Marmalade, Stripburger, Esopus, Next Level, Kasino, A4, Arkitip,Territory, Frederic Magazine, The Ganzfeld, Garageland, XFuns, Parkett, Idea, Exit, Icon, Art on Paper, Piktogram, WestEast, Clark, SWINDLE, While You Were Sleeping, Very Nearly Almost, Tokion, Bark!, Plan B, Teen Vogue, Lula, Giant Robot, Super Super Magazine, i-D, Dazed and Confused, Viewpoint, Citizen K, M-Real, Sturgeon White Moss, Raw Vision, The Comics Journal.

Websites

www.illustrationmundo.com
www.cafepress.com
www.threadless.com
www.zazzle.com
www.illustrationart.blogspot.com
www.commarts.com
www.illustrationweb.com
www.aiga.org
www.saahub.com
www.artistsbooksonline.com
www.printedmatter.org
www.onedotzero.com
www.noggallery.com
www.somagallery.co.uk
www.juxtapoz.com
www.lebook.com
www.ycnonline.com
www.bigactive.com
www.littlepaperplanes.com
www.debutart.com
www.scrawlcollective.co.uk
www.illustrationmagazine.com
www.designersblock.org.uk
www.graffitiresearchlab.com
www.heartagency.com
www.shift.jp.org

Text and Image

Title
No Sell Out
Illustrator
Mark Wigan
Description
The Dirtbox, 1984

By the author

Total Art Global Productions 1983–1993
Mark Wigan (1993)

Wig Out, drawings by Mark 'Wigan' Williams
Mark Wigan/London Institute (2003)

Amor Infinite Volume 1
Mark Wigan (2003)

Anthropology A GoGo – (A Chronicle of Cool) 1974–1984
Mark Wigan (2005)

Basics Illustration 01: Thinking Visually
AVA Publishing SA (2006)

Basics Illustration 02: Sequential Images
AVA Publishing SA (2007)

Influential Posters and Record Sleeves

Posters

Henri de Toulouse-
Lautrec
Reine de Joie
(1892)

Beggarstaff Brothers
Lyceum Don Quixote
(1895)

Alphonse Mucha
Papiera Cigarette Job
(1897)

Alfred Roller
The 16th Vienna
Secession
(1902)

John Hassall
Skegness is so Bracing
(1909)

Ernst Ludwig Kirchner
Die Brücke
(1910)

Alfred Leete
Your Country Needs You
(1914)

Lucian Bernhard
Bosch
(1915)

Edward McKnight Kauffer
Daily Herald
(1919)

Kurt Schwitters and
Theo van Doesburg
Kleine Dada Soirée
(1922)

Käthe Kollwitz
No More War
(1924)

Paul Colin
Champs-Elysées
Music Hall
(1925)

Schulz-Neudamm
Metropolis
(1926)

A.M. Cassandre
Etoile du Nord
(1927)

Alexander Rodchenko
Kino Eye
(1928)

Vladimir and
Georgii Stenberg
Man with the
Movie Camera
(1929)

John Heartfield
Adolf, the Superman,
Swallows Gold and
Spouts Tin
(1932)

Lester Beall
Rural Electrification
Administration
(1937)

Man Ray
London Transport
(1938)

Abram Games
Your Talk May Kill
Your Comrades
(1942)

Ben Shahn
This is Nazi Brutality
(1942)

Charles Loupot
St Raphaël Quinquina
(1945)

Marcello
Olivetti
(1950)

Paul Rand
No Way Out
(1950)

Tom Eckersley
General Post Office,
(1952–53)

Saul Bass
The Man with the
Golden Arm
(1955)

Text and Image

Record sleeves

Roman Cieslewicz
Vertigo
(1963)

Jan Lenica
Wozzeck
(1964)

Seymour Chwast
End Bad Breath
(1967)

Milton Glaser,
Dylan
(1967)

Peter Max
Love
(1967)

Atelier Populaire
Paris
(1968)

Tadanori Yokoo
John Silver Theatre
(1968)

Barbara Kruger
I Shop Therefore I Am,
(1987)

James Montgomery
Flagg
I Want YOU For US Army
(1917)

Art Workers Coalition
Q And Babies
A And Babies
(1970)

'Bird and Diz'
Charlie Parker
David Stone Martin
(1955)

'Mambo for Cats'
RCA Victor
Jim Flora
(1955)

'In 'n' Out'
Joe Henderson
Reid Miles
(1964)

'The Velvet Underground
and Nico'
The Velvet Underground
and Nico
Andy Warhol
(1967)

'Cheap Thrills'
Big Brother & the Holding
Company
Robert Crumb
(1968)

'Sticky Fingers'
Rolling Stones
Andy Warhol
(1971)

'Brain Salad Surgery'
Emerson, Lake & Palmer
HR Giger
(1973)

'Dark Side of the Moon'
Pink Floyd
Hipgnosis
(1973)

'God Save the Queen'
and 'Never Mind the
Bollocks'
Sex Pistols
Jamie Reid
(1977)

'Go 2'
XTC
Hipgnosis
(1978)

'Armed Forces'
Elvis Costello and
the Attractions
Barney Bubbles
(1979)

'Unknown Pleasures'
Joy Division
Peter Saville
(1979)

'Nevermind'
Nirvana
Robert Fisher
(1991)

'Set the Twilight Reeling'
Lou Reed
Stefan Sagmeister and
Veronica Oh
(1997)

'Head Music'
Suede
by Nick Knight and
Peter Saville
(1999)

Contacts

Adam Graff
a.graff@ntlworld.com
page 86

Adrian Johnson
www.adrianjohnson.org.uk
page 44

Alison Casson
alisoncasson@yahoo.com
page 128

Al Murphy
www.pocko.com
page 110

Alex Williamson
a.w.williamson@btinternet.com
pages 133, 134–135

Andrew Foster
www.ba-reps.com
page 149

Andrew Rae
www.andrewrae.org.uk
page 53, 71

Andy Potts
www.andy-potts.com
page 21

Andy Smith
andy@asmithillustration.com
page 60

Ben Freeman
www.coldhands.co.uk
page 116

Billie Jean
sam@billiejean.co.uk
pages 109, 161

Brett Ryder
www.brettryder.co.uk
page 20

Caroline Tomlinson
info@carolinetomlinson.com
page 77

Cath Elliott
www.littlegiantpictures.co.uk
page 67

Chloe King
chloeking@f25.com
page 153

Chris Watson
www.ChrisWatson.co.uk
page 148

Concrete Hermit
www.concretehermit.com
page 53

Damilola Odusote
www.damilola.com
page 157

David Foldvari
www.davidfoldvari.co.uk
pages 73

Dennis Eriksson
www.woo.se
page 73

Ed Fella
www.edfella.com
page 119

Emma Rendel
emma.rendel@alumni.rca.ac.uk
page 51

Text and Image

Graham Rawle
www.grahamrawle.com
page 56

Harry Malt
harrymalt@hotmail.com
page 79

Ian Wright
mail@mrianwright.co.uk
page 36

Jan Lenica
page 6

James Joyce
www.one-fine-day.co.uk
pages 154–155

Jason Atomic
atomicutopic@yahoo.co.uk
page 14

Jody Barton
www.jodybarton.co.uk
page 123

John Charlesworth
www.johncharlesworth.com
page 64

John Lundberg
john@circlemakers.org
page 130

John McFaul
www.mcfaul.net
pages 80–81

Jon Burgerman
www.jonburgerman.com
pages 9, 61

Jonas Bergstrand
www.jonasbergstrand.com
page 63

Jonny Hannah
jonny.sharon@virgin.net
pages 106–107, 142

Katherina Manolessou
www.lemoneyed.com
pages 54–55

Kenneth Andersson
www.kennethandersson.com
page 12

Kerry Baldry
www.kerrybaldry.moonfruit.com

Kristian Olson
www.kristianolson.com
page 23

Laura Scott
laulizscott@yahoo.co.uk
page 76

Lawrence Zeegen
z@zeegen.com
page 84

LE GUN
www.legun.co.uk
page 95, 96–97

Little White Lies
www.littlewhitelies.co.uk
page 92

Margaret Cusack
cusackart@aol.com
page 138

Marie O'Connor
Marie@peepshow.org
page 101

Margie Schnibbe
mschnibbe@earthlink.net
page 78

Mark Taplin
www.taplabs.com
page 111

Mark Wigan
www.myspace.com/markwigan
pages 08, 26–27, 28–29, 30–33
99, 144–145, 152, 169 and cover

Martin O'Neill
oneill@dircon.co.uk
page 133, 134–135

Martyn Shouler
martyn.shouler@ntlworld.com
page 129

Matt Lee
www.matt-lee.com
page 72

Michael Gillette
www.michaelgillette.com
page 88

Michelle Thompson
michellethompson.studio@
btinternet.com
page 18–19

Mr Bingo
www.mr-bingo.co.uk
page 121

Neal Fox
ammunition@legun.co.uk
page 98–99

Neasden Control Centre
www.neasdencontrolcentre.com
page 27

Nick Walker
www.apishangel.co.uk
page 126

Nishant Choksi
www.nishantchoksi.com
page 66

Olaf Hajek
www.olafhajek.com
page 29

Orly Orbach
www.orlyorbach.com
page 39

Olivier Kugler
www.olivierkugler.com
page 47

Otto Dettmer
www.ottoillustration.com
pages 54–55

Paul Bowman
bowman1@dircon.co.uk
page 49

Paul Burgess
punkrock.paul@virgin.net
page 150–151

Paul Davis
www.copyrightdavis.com
page 68–69

Paul Willoughby
www.paulwilloughby.com
page 92

Peter Arkle
www.peterarkle.com
page 43

Peter Nencini
info@peternencini.co.uk
page 100

Rachel McCow-Taylor
mail@rachelmccowattaylor.co.uk
page 128

Rian Hughes
RianHughes@aol.com
page 139

Richard Beards
Page 122

Richard May
www.richard-may.com
page 147

Rob Ryan
www.misterrob.co.uk
page 108

Russell Walker
russell@fetch.orangehome.co.uk
page 17

Salvatore Rubbino
salvatore.rubbino@alumni.rca.ac.uk
page 76

Sam Winston
www.samwinston.com
page 137

Serge Seidlitz
www.sergeseidlitz.com
pages 24–25, 81

Si Scott
www.siscottdesign.com
page 75

Simon Taylor
www.tomato.co.uk
page 127

Simone Lia
www.simonelia.com
page 159

Spencer Wilson
www.spencerwilson.co.uk
page 87

Stephen Fowler
page 89

Susanna Edwards
dapper@tesco.net
pages 124–125

The Illustrated Ape
www.theillustratedape.com
page 90

The Mangle/Dan Holliday
themangle@excite.com
page 146

UHC
www.uhc.org.uk
pages 102–103, 104–105

Zoe Taylor
zlysbeth@hotmail.com
pages 40–41

Acknowledgements

John Ruskin stated that 'industry without art is brutality', a comment never more valid than now as our world moves into a new paradigm of uncertainty, anxiety and unprecedented technological change. The illustrator brings art to commerce and industry, raises questions, embraces technology and illuminates human experience.

Many thanks to the contributors who, with their own unique *modus operandi* and points of view, challenge preconceptions of the discipline. Your intelligent, oblique, beguiling, visceral and life-affirming images reflect the strength and diversity of contemporary practice. Also many thanks to artist Kerry Baldry for the many hours she has spent compiling information and researching.

I am also indebted to my colleagues in academe for their loyal support and *esprit de corps*. Keep upholding academic freedom, independent thought, diverse approaches to education and the joy of learning in our art schools.

A special thanks is due to the graphic design staff and students at Coventry University whom I had the pleasure of working with. I would also like to acknowledge the dedication and professionalism of my staff teams on the BA (Hons) Illustration and MA Illustration at Camberwell College of Arts and the BA (Hons) Graphic Design Programme at The University of Salford.

And finally thank you to Caroline Walmsley, Brian Morris, Sanaz Nazemi at AVA Publishing, and to Darren Lever for the book's page and cover design.

Text and Image